IMAGES
of America

LAKE VILLA TOWNSHIP

ILLINOIS

IMAGES
of America

LAKE VILLA TOWNSHIP
ILLINOIS

Joseph W. Brysiewicz

ARCADIA

Published by Arcadia Publishing,
an imprint of Tempus Publishing, Inc.
3047 N. Lincoln Ave., Suite 410
Chicago, IL 60657

Printed in Great Britain.

Library of Congress Catalog Card Number: 2001092768

For all general information contact Arcadia Publishing at:
Telephone 843-853-2070
Fax 843-853-0044
E-Mail sales@arcadiapublishing.com

For customer service and orders:
Toll-Free 1-888-313-2665

Visit us on the internet at http://www.arcadiapublishing.com

Contents

ACKNOWLEDGMENTS

Like any project of this nature, there are many people who were crucial in this book's creation. As a result, some that have contributed to the success of this project may be omitted here. I offer my apologies in advance.

First and foremost, this book would have been impossible without the shared photographs and stories of many local residents. Bill and Carol Effinger, Tom and Sharon Barnstable, Robert and Shawn Frank (courtesy of Infinity Web Design), Ms. Garcia and Mayor Paul Baumunk at the Lindenhurst Village Hall, and Kelly Ewalt and Lawrence Clayton at the Lake Villa District Library offered both photographs and stories that comprise the substance of this book.

To those who generously donated their time to be interviewed: Marlene Coia, Dorothy Langbein, Jim Streicher, Amelia Saxe, Anna Stout, Patricia Tranberg, and Aja Brown, I give a sincere thanks. I especially want to thank Candace Saunders, Julie Kloc Trychta, and Michael Polsgrove for their highest scholarship and the fruitful yield of their labor. I am particularly indebted to Ms. Saunders, without whom the Lehmann family chapter could never have been written.

I would also like to thank those mentors who pushed me for the best possible product: Professor Steven Rosswurm, Art Miller, and especially Professor Michael Ebner, whose assistance was crucial in the larger vision of this work. To Erin Lucido and David Hain, for their incisive editing suggestions. Also, I would like to thank Rose Imaging Center for their professional, prompt, and courteous response to my somewhat outrageous requests.

Finally, I would like to thank my family: Walter, Gwen, and Neil Brysiewicz for their unwavering support during a process that at times eclipsed all else in my life. And to Beth Johnson, whose thoughtful remarks, encouragement, companionship, and willingness to be a sounding board were invaluable. I can only say thank you. In spite of the generous assistance from the above people, any errors contained within this work are solely mine.

INTRODUCTION

To understand Lake Villa Township's history, it is important to look at its prehistory, including the area's geology and geography. Geographically, the township is approximately 53 miles northwest of Chicago's loop, 4 miles south of the Wisconsin border, and 13 miles west of Lake Michigan. The whole area is replete with lakes, stands of trees, prairies, and swamps. One early catalog of this natural landscape can be found in the journal of Colonel C. Benton, an amateur explorer who came from the East Coast and traveled north through central Lake County. One night he allegedly stopped on the banks of Cedar Lake, and his journal describes much of the land as savannah, marsh, and wet prairie. Though the township area consisted of land questionably suited for agriculture (this is not to discount the many small farms that did exist), its geography and proximity to Chicago did lend the potential for habitation, industry, and recreation. The effects of Chicago's proximity should not be underestimated. William Cronon, a scholar of the Midwest, analyzes the importance of what he calls the "hinterland:" the outlying land of a city is as integral as its urban center in understanding a metropolitan region. Conversely, knowledge of the city creates a better understanding of the hinterland.

Though important, geography and vegetation are not the only considerations of environment. Knowledge of Lake Villa Township's geology, specifically the influence of the Valparaiso Moraine, is also essential. Geologically, all of what is today metropolitan Chicago (including Lake Villa) was created in its present form by the recession of glaciers between 14,000 and 13,000 years ago. The retreat of glacial ice during this period is primarily responsible for the production of the area's varied topography. This terrain includes the many lakes formed by blocks of glacial ice wedged in the soil and the mounds of soil left by the glacier's retreat. Specifically, the township is part of the Valparaiso Moraine, a ridge of glacial material surrounding Lake Michigan in a concentric fashion. Quite large, it stretches well into Wisconsin and around Lake Michigan into Indiana and Michigan. In general, the Valparaiso Moraine stands 12 miles beyond Lake Michigan and ranges in height from 100 to 500 feet in elevation. Throughout the region, this moraine is characterized by a highly irregular surface caused by pockets of glacial ice. This surface is the foundation of the village's many lakes and hills. The island in Cedar Lake and the high banks of Deep Lake are examples of glacial deposits, while the 10 major lakes in and around Lake Villa are a testament to the effects of glacial recession.

In a way, Lake Villa's success as a resort community was almost entirely created out of this glacial terrain's recreational appeal. In terms of specificity, a history of Lake Villa published in 1918 provides the most detailed description of its natural history. Written by Edna Wallace, a student in the Lake Villa School system, it honored the occasion of Illinois' statehood centennial. For the anniversary, seventh and eighth graders compiled a history under the supervision of their teacher, Alice Smith. It includes a section on geology:

> It is evident also that the soil was formed by the glacier, for most of the soil in the town of Lake Villa is yellow-gray silt loam, which is a glacial soil. It has the characteristic billowy appearance, which is a feature of moraines. This soil is deficient in organic matter and needs nitrogen and ground limestone for the most profitable agriculture. A small part of the soil is yellow silt loam, which occurs in the highest part of the Valparaiso Moraine, and is due to the piling up of the material.

The foregoing also explains how the area's geology created less than adequate farming soil. It seems that Lake Villa, the hinterland of Chicago, could never be a great agricultural center in the Midwest. Yet, the very birth of Lake Villa was agricultural. With these beginnings, the village had little to offer the surrounding region, and to a large extent, Lake Villa Township was understandably isolated from Chicago. This path would change once the village's natural resources were utilized differently. Eventually, its geographic strength was put to advantage— its lakes. Though it began quietly, Lake Villa Township eventually exploded as a popular resort area. It would become the "Gateway to the Lakes Region."

Like most rapid ascents, however, the resorting boom of Lake Villa Township declined with time. Through most of the 20th century, Lake Villa Township gradually lost its influence as a great resort haven away from Chicago. This book is a pictorial and historical journey following the rise, fall, and future of this important point in the greater metropolitan Chicago region. As a note, all photographs are credited to the Lake Villa District Library unless otherwise noted. For a more detailed look at the sources I have utilized throughout my research, please read *Lake Villa, Illinois: Constructing Multiple Narratives on Chicago's Metropolitan Fringe.*

Joe W. Brysiewicz

One
PIONEER SPIRIT

In 1845, Mr. Manzer went to the county seat to borrow money for a neighbor who was in trouble.
A severe storm came on; it was winter—and in the morning he was found frozen to death within a
mile from his home. . . .

—1918 History of Lake Villa

M r. Christopher Manzer, whose untimely end is recounted above from a 1918 local history, was one of the original four men to settle in what would eventually become Lake Villa Township. His tragic story reveals one element of the dangerous, isolated life early European-descended settlers faced in this region. After the U.S. government successfully wrested control of northern Illinois away from Native Americans, men and women from as far away as England bought claims from the government. With these claims, many families started a new agrarian existence, far from their old homes, even isolated by as much as a week from Chicago.

Throughout the 19th century, these early settlers created self-sufficient communities to combat isolation and hardship. Lake Villa Township did not exist: this distinction did not arise until as late as 1913. Rather, a series of early communities such as Monaville, Angola, Sand Lake, and eventually Lake Villa built homes, schools, and churches. In the process, these small trading posts developed a sense of shared identity while uniquely defining the hinterland of a burgeoning city.

Rural isolation, however, could not last forever. Though Monaville began as the most prominent community of the early township region, a small community to its north, Stanwood, began to attract more and more settlers in the early 1880s. In particular, a wealthy Chicago investor and businessman, Ernst Johann Lehmann, took a special interest in Stanwood. Buying just 300 acres in 1883, Lehmann renamed the small Stanwood Post Office Lake Villa, and opened the lavish 150-room Lake Villa Hotel. With its myriad lakes, Lehmann was not the first to open a resort in the township region. Many small family-run resorts were already in business by the time he had arrived. Nevertheless, Lehmann's money and power did manage to bring something to Lake Villa that put an end to both Monaville as well as the isolated nature of the region—the railroad.

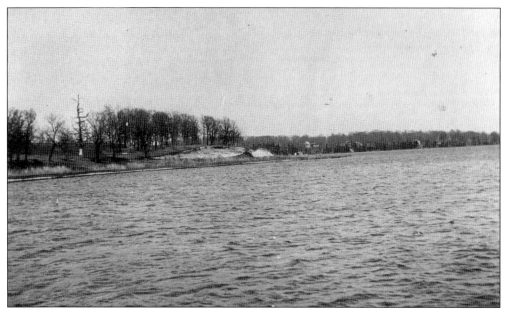

The many lakes (at least 10 naturally occurring) of Lake Villa Township reveal evidence of glacial recession. Both the high gravel banks of Deep Lake and the island on Cedar Lake are indicators of past glacial activity. According to a 1918 student history, even the area's soil displays its effects. "It is evident also that the soil was formed by the glacier, for most of the soil in the town of Lake Villa is yellow-gray silt loam, which is a glacier soil."

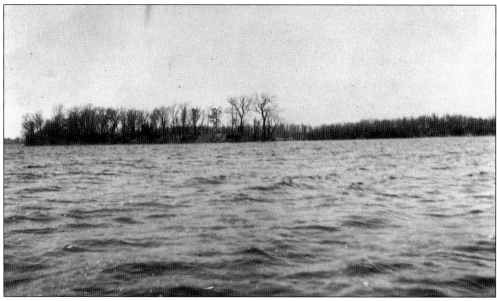

This is an early photograph of Cedar Lake showing Cedar Island. The island may have served as a recognizable landmark for early white travelers such as Colbee C. Benton. In his *Journal to the Far-Off West* (1830s), Benton remarks, "There is a small island in the lake which the Indians said was covered with small pines, but I was not able to distinguish them, it was so far from the shore. The lake was surrounded by oak openings, had a stony bottom, and the water looked very clear indeed."

10

Before white settlers came to the area, Native Americans, primarily Potawatomi, populated the township. After a series of treaties between the U.S. and the Sauk, Blackhawk, and Potawatomi in the 1830s, most vacated the region and headed west past the Mississippi. Even so, many artifacts such as these arrowheads and spears continued to be "plowed up in the region" long after the Native Americans had gone.

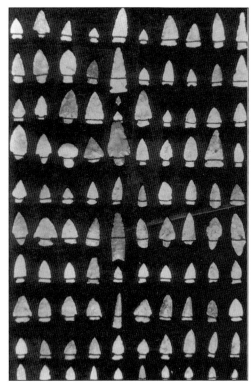

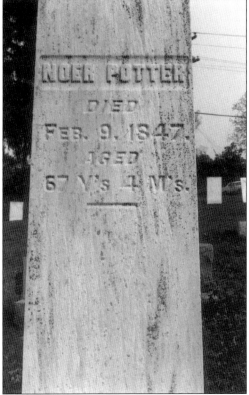

In 1837, Noer Potter and his son Tingley came from Pennsylvania and established the first area farmstead around the present-day intersection of Monaville Road and Route 83. Later that same year, Noer Potter's other son Ira arrived with Christopher Manzer, who established another farmstead directly north of the Potter property. Ten years later, Lake Villa Township's first white settler was laid to rest in Angola Cemetery.

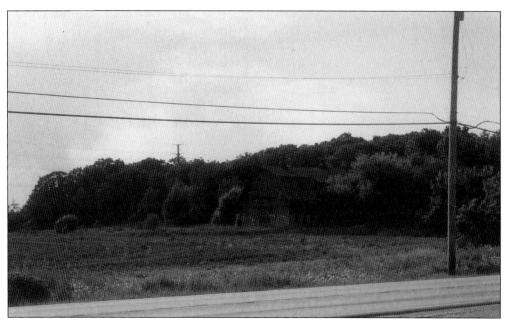

Though much of the earliest settlement in the township has been erased by constant development over the last 150 years, some relics of the past still remain. This decrepit barn on the west side of Route 83 stands on what was one of the original tracts of government land given to European settlers. (Photograph by author.)

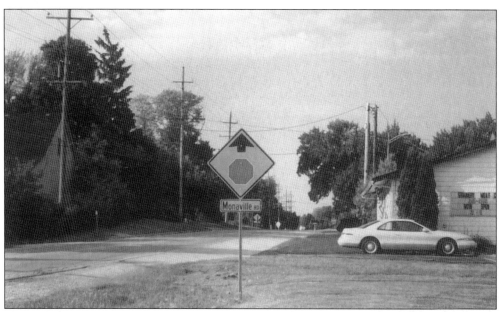

Monaville was the name given to the first significant point of trade and post within Lake Villa Township. Many of its settlers were from the town of Mona on the Isle of Man in England, hence the community's appellation. In addition to these settlers from across the Atlantic, a large group of Somerset immigrants also settled farms in Monaville. Currently on the southern end of Lake Villa, all that remains today of this early community is its namesake road. (Photograph by author.)

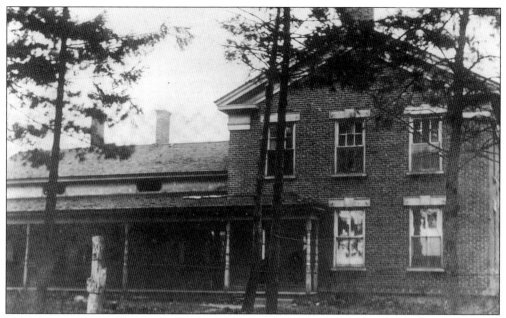

Despite the prominence of Monaville throughout the middle of the 19th century, early settlers directly north of the community also thrived. In particular, Stephen Sherwood prospered by running a brickyard—and having over 17 children, according to an 1877 history of Lake County. Owning the whole southern half of what would become the Village of Lake Villa, Sherwood's impressive brick home stood on the northwestern corner of Route 132 and Route 83, the current home of Joseph J. Pleviak School.

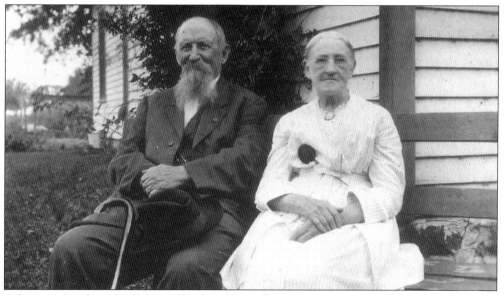

Other men lived north of Monaville, though not all were as prominent as Sherwood. Mr. Mason Douglas (pictured next to his wife c. 1917) was a veteran of the Civil War. Of the many men from the area who fought in this war, Mr. Douglas was one of the few to survive. Like most of those who did survive, he resettled in the township after the war's conclusion. Russ Douglas, presumably Mr. Douglas's son, eventually became the railroad agent for the Village of Lake Villa.

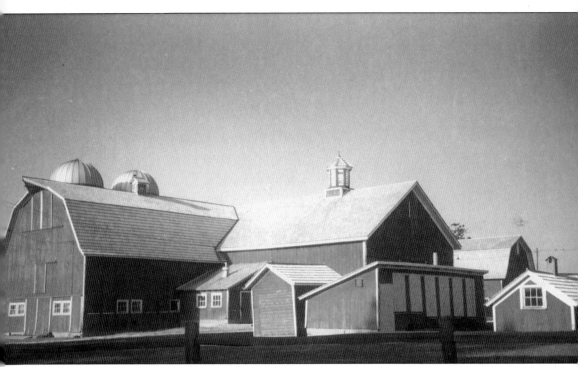

On the eastern end of the township, the post office of Sand Lake drew together a small community of farmers, blacksmiths, and other tradesman. This 1842 farmstead was owned by the Bonner family for many generations and was active until the 1990s. As the Chicago metropolitan area expands, land in Lake Villa Township has been increasingly desirable to many developers. For local farmers, selling their land to developers is advantageous to continued farming. Though the Bonner farm has since become Country Place subdivision, the Lake County Forest Preserve has purchased the home and various original farm structures. Aside from restoring these structures, there are tentative plans to convert the Bonner farm into a museum. (Photograph by author.)

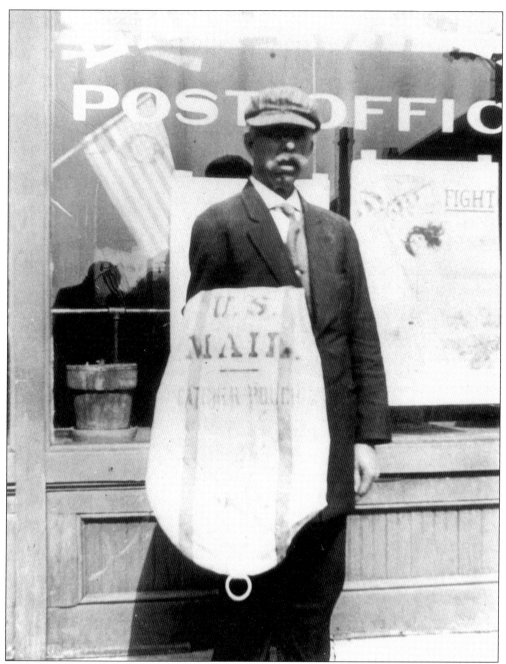

Frank G. Hooper was the region's mail carrier for many years, even before the existence of a Lake Villa post office. Hooper's original route made stops at Monaville, Angola (changed to Sand Lake in 1863), Millburn, Gurnee, and Waukegan. Hooper would only make this trip twice a week. In a testament to the isolation of the early township, many local farmers such as Herman Hall found it necessary to get a ride from Hooper in order to travel to Waukegan (from where the railroad brought many to Chicago). Hall mentions getting a ride from Hooper on multiple occasions in a journal he kept during the 1880s. This particular photograph must have been taken after August 21, 1886, the date of the creation of the Lake Villa Post Office.

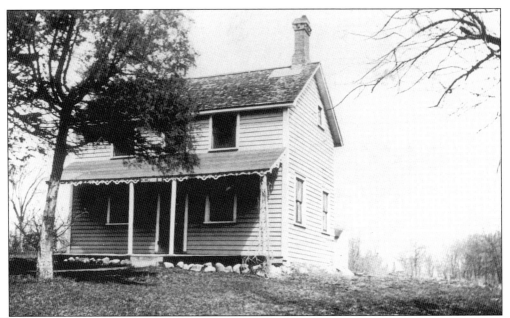

On the western end of the township, Gustavus Farnsworth bought land from the government for $1.25 an acre. A community "common" ran along to the south and west of Farnsworth's property where cows could freely graze. According to the 1918 history, "Each family had a cow-bell on one cow of its herd, and all the cow-bells were of different tone. The Farnsworths are said to have owned the best and most musical bell." Gustavus's daughter, Elizabeth Doolittle, was one of the original teachers at Angola School.

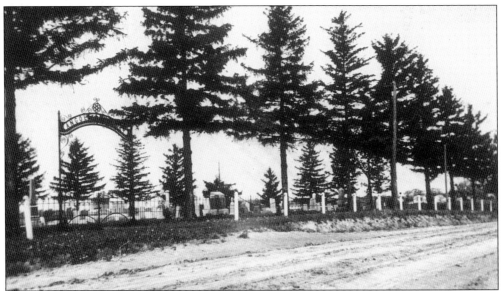

Angola Cemetery, just south of the intersection of Route 83 and Route 132, is one of the earliest markers of European settlement in the area. Formally designated as a cemetery in 1840, Angola has retained its original condition, thanks largely to dedicated caretakers over the years, particularly the Cribb family. Of all the cemeteries in the township, Angola harbors the earliest burial, which was Fannie Parker in 1842.

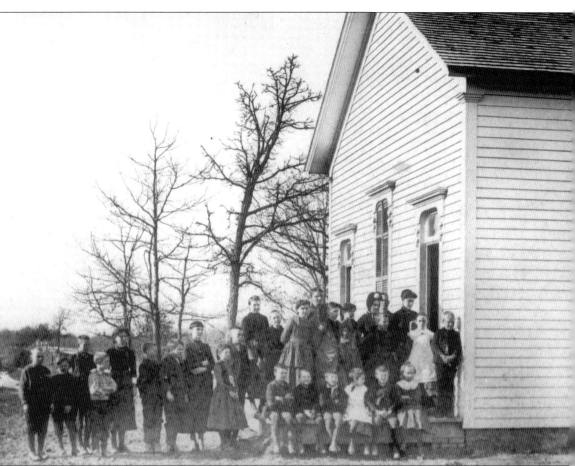

Though both Monaville and Sand Lake constructed schoolhouses before the Village of Lake Villa area, Angola School was built on the eastern side of Route 83 in 1845, directly across from Angola Cemetery. No record of names seems to exist with this picture, but the 1918 history of the area mentions many of the first Angola schoolteachers, such as Charlotte Miller; Sarah, Ruth, and Sophia Dennick; Ellen Warner; as well as Henry Sherwood. Directly behind this original school was a small pond that proved to be "an unfailing source of pleasure to the pupils." This one-room schoolhouse operated until it was struck by lightning on an August afternoon in 1898 and burnt down. This is a photograph of the 1886 class of Angola School, taken in March of that year.

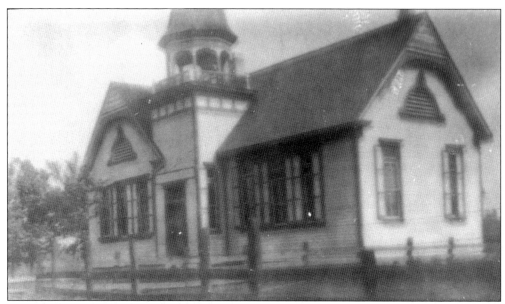

After the destruction of the first schoolhouse, a second was built on the same site at the turn of the century. Unlike the old structure, however, the new school boasted three rooms, furnace heat, and cloakrooms, as well as a basement. In the first years of the 20th century, only three staff members ran the school; Mr. Felkner was principal, his wife was the teacher of primary students, and Miss Darley was the teacher of intermediate students. Despite the amenities and relative modernity of this school, it burnt down like the first on the night of April 10, 1909.

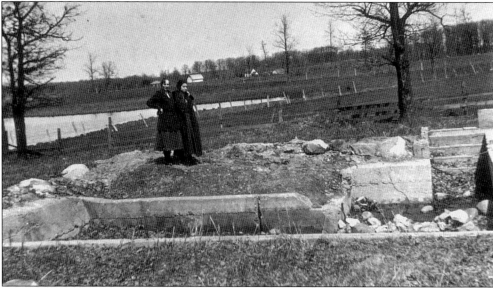

The 1909 destruction of the schoolhouse marked the end of Angola School. By 1900, older settlements such as Monaville were eclipsed by the growing prominence of Lake Villa to the north. When the time came for a third schoolhouse to be built for area children, it was renamed Lake Villa School and located farther north, on the northwest corner of Route 83 and 132. In this photograph, two women observe the remnants of Angola School. Note the "school pond" behind the women.

Though the township area built many schoolhouses from the onset, the construction of a permanent church did not take place until 1876 (though a parsonage was built in Sand Lake by 1858). On December 14, 1876, the First Methodist Episcopal Church of the Town of Avon was dedicated on L.C. Manzer's property, approximately a mile south of the intersection of Route 83 and Route 132. In 1892, the church was torn down and reassembled in the burgeoning village of Lake Villa, at the intersection of Cedar Avenue and Route 83.

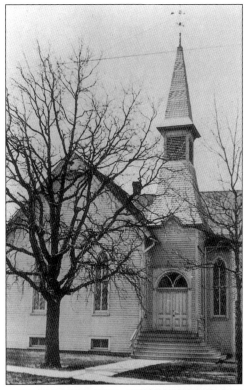

The interior of this church displays a relatively high architectural aesthetic for the rural atmosphere of the Lake Villa Township area. The sober wooden pews complement the beautiful windows and vaulted ceiling of this early Lake Villa church. Of note is the wide central division between the pews. In the early days of this church, men were most likely seated on one side while women were seated on the other.

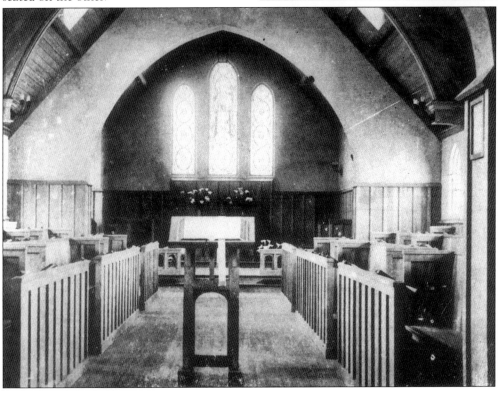

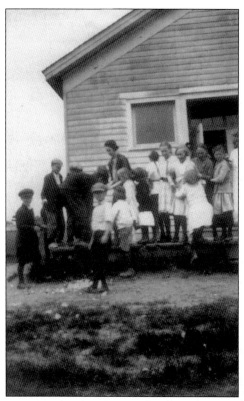

In operation by at least 1841, Monaville School was one of the first municipal buildings in the Lake Villa Township area. With plank desks and seats, this schoolhouse was also utilized as a site for Sunday school, church, choir lessons, and the East Fox Lake Cemetery Society. Mary Kerr is the teacher in this photograph. (Courtesy of Tom and Sharon Barnstable.)

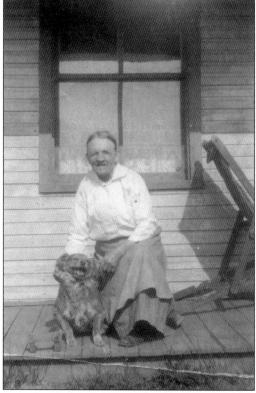

Labeled "Gramma and Sport," this woman is possibly Charity Sorenson, related to the Tweed family. Even today, her family lineage includes many prominent local families such as the Barnstables. Quite elderly in this early 20th century photograph, her visage is a glimpse into the dress and lifestyle of early township settlers. (Courtesy of Tom and Sharon Barnstable.)

Shown here feeding chickens, "Gramma" is literally wrapped up to fight against harsh weather. Early settler Herman Hall makes numerous references to the weather, both friend and foe to the isolated agrarian. (Courtesy of Tom and Sharon Barnstable.)

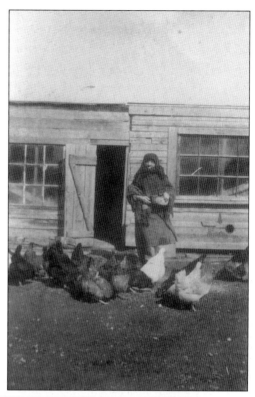

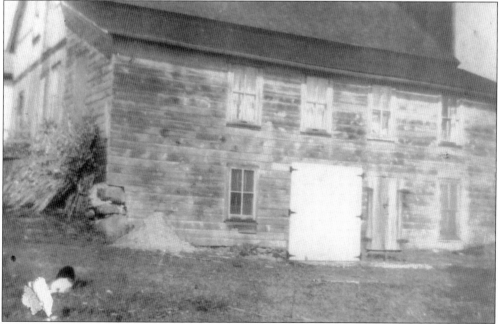

The Tweed store, located at the intersection of Fairfield and Monaville Roads, was a major source of general merchandise in the settlement of Monaville. For a time, it simultaneously served as the post office when Alexander Tweed was made the area postmaster in 1882. (Courtesy of Tom and Sharon Barnstable.)

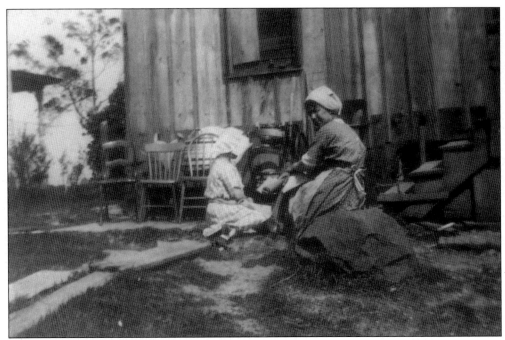

The woman and girl in this photograph are cleaning, according to the photograph's original caption. Though the responsibilities and occupations of early male settlers are often noted for posterity, women shouldered a large brunt of the work necessary to maintain prosperity on the frontier. (Courtesy of Tom and Sharon Barnstable.)

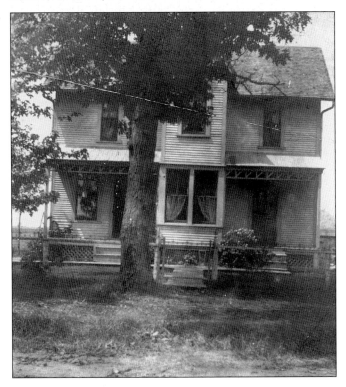

The Charles Hamlin home is one of the oldest in the township area. Eventually it was sold to Harry Stratton whose relative, John Stratton, would become the first supervisor of Lake Villa Township in 1913. The Hamlin family was one of the earliest to the area, and around the turn of the century built most of the Lehmann estates.

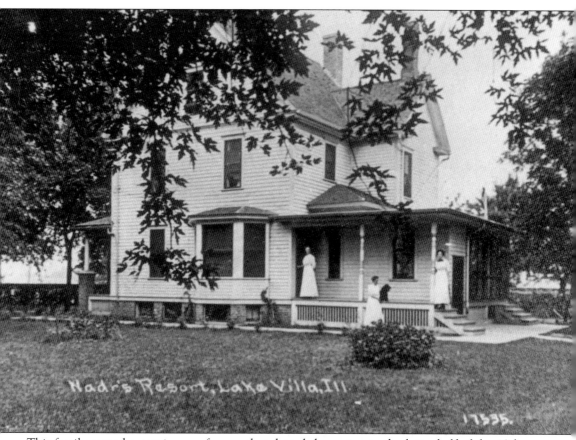

Nadr's Resort, Lake Villa, Ill.

This family-owned resort is one of many that dotted the region in the latter half of the 19th century. Predominately an agrarian area (105 out of 120 homesteads in 1877 were farms), the many lakes of the township and location out of Chicago fostered the development of small vacation resorts. Nevertheless, erratic stagecoach schedules and unreliable transportation prohibited these resorts from growing into larger operations. These businesses did, however, foreshadow the resort industry boom that Lake Villa would eventually experience at the hands of Ernst J. Lehmann.

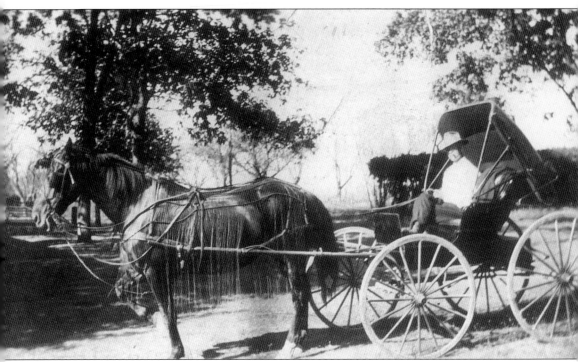

In the early days of Lake Villa Township, isolation and self-sufficiency were the keystones to survival for those who settled on these former Potawatomi lands. Only a few settlers, such as Charles Hucker pictured here, owned a horse. Monaville, Angola, Sand Lake, and Lake Villa were communities that relied on one another to ensure enough goods and services were available to all. The October 11, 1884 entry to Herman Hall's journal reveals this pioneer spirit: "Commenced siding. Sided west side (of friend's barn). Put on half cow shed roof. Commenced laying floor. . . ." Though the region inevitably modernized as the 19th century came to a close, its foundation lay in the toil and solidarity of its earliest settlers. (Courtesy of Bill and Carol Effinger.)

Two

RAILS AND RESORTS

Being on the railroad attracted new businesses to (Lake Villa). This caused a slow decline in the business at Monaville. Nothing new was built. Some businesses left for the railroad towns, and soon after the moving of the Fox Lake Post Office to Ingleside, there was only the butter factory and Tom Nelson's Blacksmith Shop.

—Raymond Walsh

Lake Villa Township's first settlers led an agrarian existence. By the time of Herman Hall's journal, however, things had already begun to change. When Herman wrote in 1884, it was almost 50 years after Noer Potter and sons had made the area's first claim. By Hall's time, farmers, blacksmiths, and even a few wealthy speculators had claimed most of the township's land. In particular, one wealthy entrepreneur was in the process of bringing radical change to the area: Ernst Johann Lehmann.

In 1884, the Monaville trading post seemed to be the obvious choice for a railroad stop. It had an established post office and a small aggregate of businesses. In his February 9, 1884 journal entry, Hall mentions a railroad survey through Monaville. The Wisconsin Central Railroad Company was interested in bringing a new rail line through the area.

Lehmann, who had purchased land to the north of Monaville that he would later name Lake Villa, desired the train line to come through his resort. On October 28, 1885, Lehmann sold easement property to the Wisconsin Central Railroad Company for the price of $1. Problems plagued the construction of the railroad. Nevertheless, July 26, 1886 marked the first day of train service, linking Lake Villa directly with Chicago.

Though this turn of events brought the demise of Monaville and Sand Lake, the resorting industry of the region exploded as a result of the train. The myriad lakes in the area and the new accessibility to privileged urbanites guaranteed a new status to the Village of Lake Villa. By 1901, Lake Villa was incorporated; by 1913, the village carved a new township out of southern Antioch Township, northern Avon Township, and eastern Grant Township. Even though this area included the once thriving Monaville, Angola, and Sand Lake, it was appropriately dubbed Lake Villa Township.

CHICAGO IS A WONDERFUL CITY,

And the most wonderful Wonder which it contains is

The Fair

-- of --

E. J. LEHMANN,

Which is like unto

A Ten Acre Lot Covered Several Feet Deep with Merchandise

of every conceivable description, brought from every clime under the sun, and sold at

LESS THAN MANUFACTURERS' PRICES.

This

PEERLESS PALACE OF PRODUCE

is the most popular retail trading place in America, and is the

Largest Variety Store on Earth,

It is fitted up with all the modern improvements and conveniences and is daily visited by

THOUSANDS OF STRANGERS AND CITIZENS.

Who unite in proclaiming it

The Greatest Attraction in the City.

In its sixty different stores, which are all under one roof and one management, can be found

EXHIBITS FROM ALL PARTS OF THE WORLD,

thus giving it undisputed right to the title of "The Fair," containing as it does more attractions than are usually found at

A Dozen Ordinary Fairs.

Persons living within a radius of fifty miles of Chicago can save enough money on a ten dollar purchase by

TAKING ADVANTAGE of "FAIR PRICES"

as compared with prices offered at other stores, to pay their expenses to and from the city. No
visitor to Chicago can afford to miss calling at this

Great Business Bazaar,

and viewing the miniature world of trade. **THE ARMY OF CLERKS** and other employees together with the endless corridors
lined with a wealth of merchandise, rivaling in extent and elegance the magnificent scenes pictured in the
famous Arabian Nights Tales. All of the articles forming this **GORGEOUS DISPLAY** are for sale
at astonishingly low prices. Bear in mind that the only place in the world where
this **SUPERB MERCANTILE PANORAMA**, including everything known to
trade, whether for agricultural, horticultural or domestic
use, can be seen, is at

THE FAIR

-- of --

E. J. LEHMANN,

which fronts on three leading business thoroughfares.

STATE, ADAMS & DEARBORN STREETS,
CHICAGO, - - ILLINOIS.

Ernst J. Lehmann opened the Fair Store in 1875, on the west side of State Street, just 16 feet north of Adams Street. At the time, the store was 1,280 square feet. Catering to the working class and creating many innovative marketing strategies such as broken nickel pricing, Lehmann's store became a great success. As his fortune grew, the Fair aggressively incorporated neighboring shops and stores. By 1897, only 14 years after its opening, the store was 677,500 square feet, 9 stories high, and encompassed the whole block bounded by Dearborn Street, Adams Street, State Street, and an alleyway. The astonishing success of Lehmann's business ventures allowed him to explore business opportunities outside the city of Chicago. (Courtesy of Paul R. Getz Foundation.)

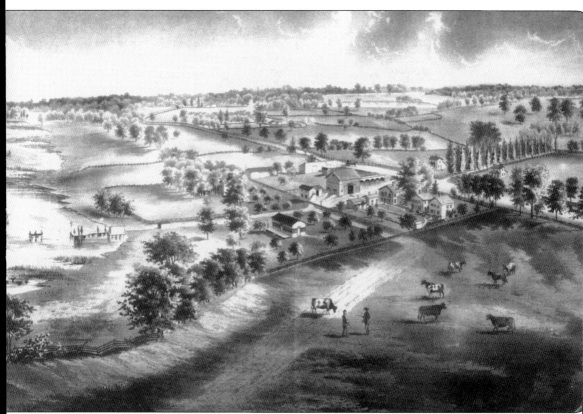

This 1885 illustration displays the 300-acre Stewart farm, Stanwood, which E.J. Lehmann made his summer home in 1883. Before the railroad, this illustration shows Antioch Road (Route 83) running through the estate. Located just north of present day Route 132, the estate rested on the eastern shore of Cedar Lake. Toward the bottom of the illustration, a precursor to Cedar Avenue runs away from Lehmann's estate into what would eventually become downtown Lake Villa. At this point, however, Monaville was still the leading community of the area, and Lake Villa was nonexistent. (Courtesy of Paul R. Getz Foundation.)

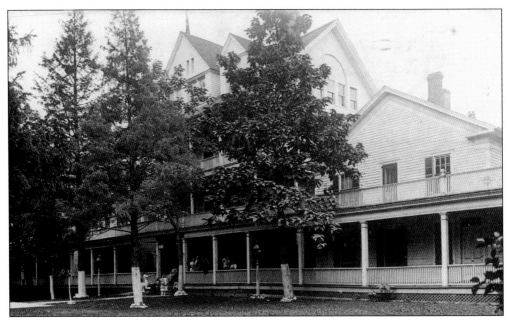

E.J. Lehmann continued the operations of the large resort on the Stewart farm. Naming it the Lake City Hotel and then the Lake Villa Hotel, Lehmann invited many business associates and friends from Chicago to stay at his new resort. Furthermore, employees of the Fair Store were given the opportunity to stay at Lehmann's hotel for the reduced rate of $1 a day.

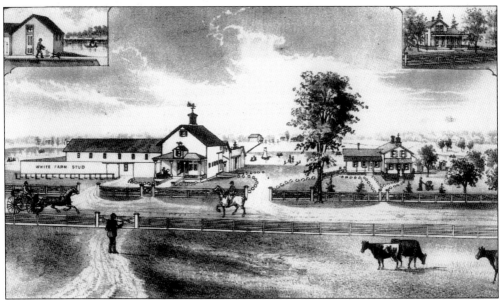

E.J. Lehmann was not the only resident who had a large gentleman estate. William Emmett owned the opulent White Farm. Located on the shore of Sand Lake, Emmett raised and raced horses, allowed access to Sand Lake for those willing to pay, and ran a small resort business where people passing through could stay. (Courtesy of Paul R. Getz Foundation.)

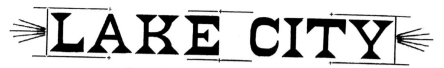
This 1885 advertisement for the Lake City Hotel extols the resort's "Picturesque Scenes, Romantic Ravines, Historic Hills Beautiful Lakes, Lovely Lawns, Mammoth Oaks, and more extensive Hunting and Fishing grounds, than all the other advertised resorts combined." More significant are the two branches of the Lake City Hotel advertised here. With one in Gurnee and the other in Fox Lake, Lehmann created a line of hotels along an east-west route directly from the Waukegan train station. As a result, the wealthy entrepreneur started the first dependable stagecoach line from Waukegan to Lake Villa, signaling the end of regional isolation. (Courtesy of Paul R. Getz Foundation.)

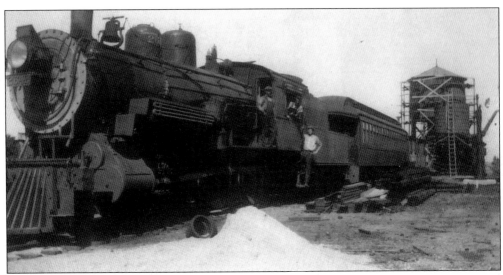

The real end of Lake Villa Township's isolation came with the arrival of the Wisconsin Central in 1886. Purchasing Lake Villa right of way for $1 from E.J. Lehmann, the Wisconsin Central Railroad Company bypassed Monaville all together. Rumor has it (no known evidence exists) that Lehmann sold the property at discount to Wisconsin Central in return for a guarantee that every passenger train on the line would stop in Lake Villa. (Courtesy of Tom and Sharon Barnstable.)

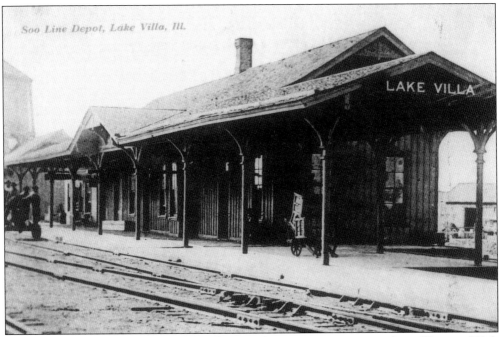

The Lake Villa Depot was created for the use of passengers coming up from Chicago. With direct and rapid access to Chicago, resorting in Lake Villa exploded after 1886. It is speculated that Lehmann's property in Lake View (a community directly north of Chicago now incorporated into the city) rose in value when a railway came through the community. It is possible that he planned to duplicate this financial gain in Lake Villa.

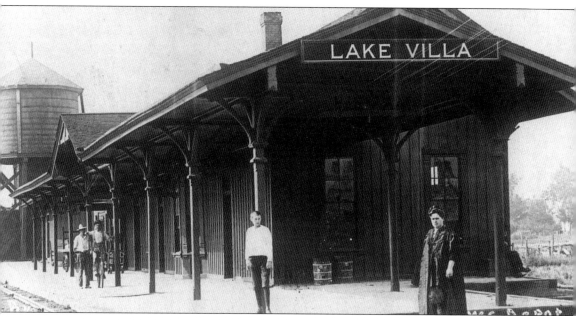

This is a photograph of the train depot looking south. This particular image served as a postcard for the area during Lake Villa's resort boom at the turn of the century. In the background is the water tank that was used to refill steam locomotives passing through the community. During its early years, the depot required a day operator. At the time this photograph was taken, that job belonged to an Otto Lake. George Sugar is riding a bicycle in this photograph, and W.R. Kerr is the man standing beside him. Both the Kerrs and the Sugars owned businesses on Cedar Avenue during this time period. (Courtesy of Bill and Carol Effinger.)

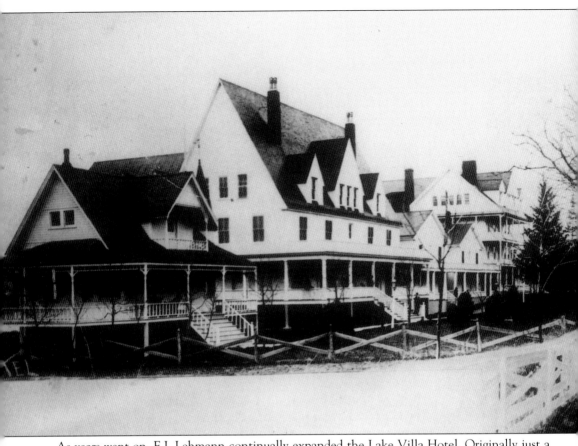

As years went on, E.J. Lehmann continually expanded the Lake Villa Hotel. Originally just a large family-run resort, it eventually became a major resort complex boasting over 150 rooms. Though many resorts dotted the township region following the railroad, Lehmann's Lake Villa Hotel was truly the centerpiece of Lake Villa's vacation appeal. This is a photograph of the primary hotel on the multi-facility complex.

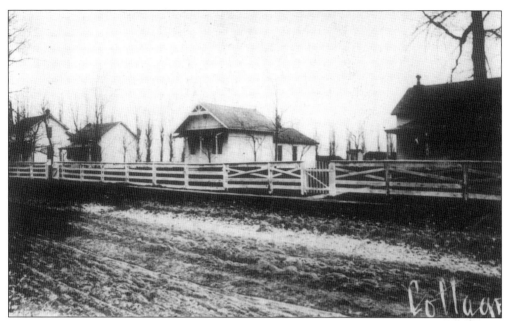

The Lake Villa Hotel, however, was grander than just a single large resort building. Lehmann added many small guest cottages to line Cedar Lake, giving a more private and home-like atmosphere for longer stays. Other perks for the pampered guests of E.J. Lehmann's resort included beach access, countryside sightseeing wagon tours, and hiking, hunting, and fishing privileges for patrons.

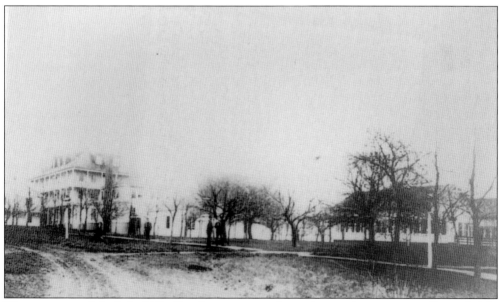

The amenities of the Lake Villa Hotel were not just limited to outdoor activities. For nightlife, Lehmann's resort complex included a dance hall on Deep Lake, a large fine dining facility, even the bowling alley pictured here. For a region so recently submerged in agrarian isolation, this grand hotel offered infinite possibilities.

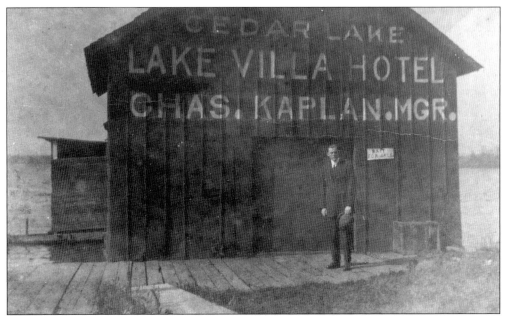

Of all the attractions offered by the Lake Villa Hotel, the most popular seems to have been the circular club built on Cedar Island. With both casino gambling and alcohol readily available, the island club was a major part of the Lake Villa Hotel experience. The resort offered paddleboats to service guests to and from the island. Wendell Laguess, caretaker of the Lake Villa Hotel Boathouse posed for this 1914 photograph. (Courtesy of Bill and Carol Effinger.)

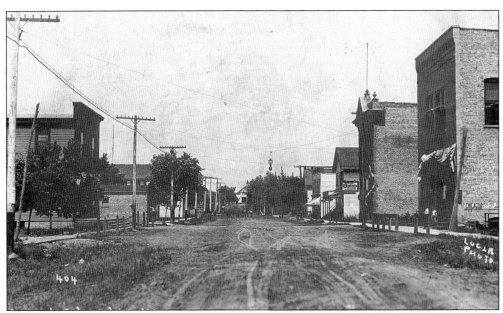

E.J. Lehmann's grand resort complex had many other effects on the surrounding region. The Village of Lake Villa sprang up in the span of a short decade. This view of Cedar Avenue reveals late 19th century downtown Lake Villa. As late as the 1870s, only a handful of farmsteads occupied the area that would become the "downtown triangle" (Cedar Avenue, Route 132, and Route 83).

This is a photograph of James Kerr's hardware and general merchandise store, one of the first businesses in the new downtown of Lake Villa. The following people are pictured in this photograph (the exact order has been lost, though most guess the following from left to right): Doc Morell, Johnnie McMahon, James Kerr, Edgar Kerr, Bill Cremin, and Jack the Tinner. (Courtesy of Bill and Carol Effinger.)

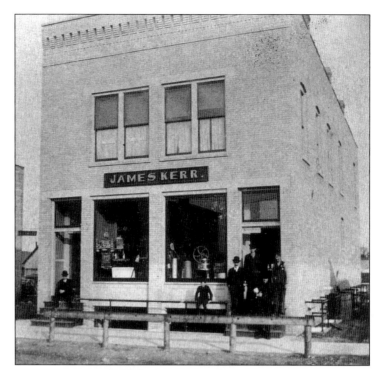

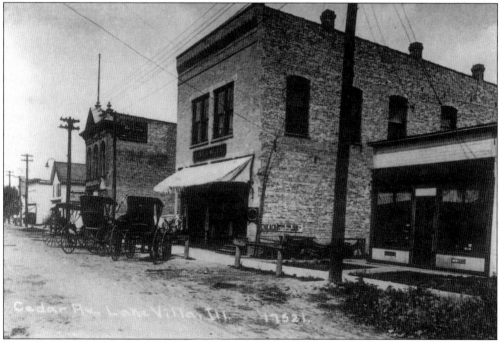

The downtown of Lake Villa was different in many respects from the earlier pioneer communities of the township. For example, James Kerr's store served a similar function of the Tweed store in Monaville. In Kerr's store, however, Fred Hamlin ran a pool hall in the basement during the early part of the 20th century. Later, James Kerr went into business with a Mr. Avery, as is noted on the store front in this photograph.

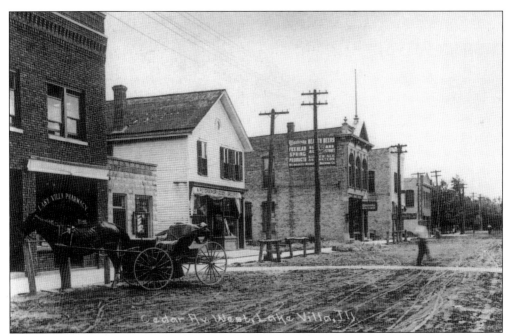

Many other businesses grew around the sudden explosion of the Lake Villa Hotel. The Lake Villa Pharmacy, a barbershop, and Petersen's dry good grocery store line the streets in this photograph. In addition to the railroad, this new and relatively sudden concentration of business in Lake Villa made it difficult for Monaville to thrive commercially.

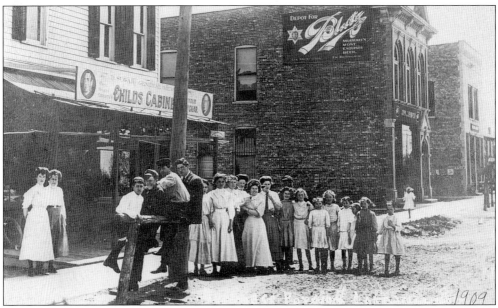

In this new downtown business district, turnover was both more common and more frequent. This photograph, taken a few years before the one above, shows the predecessor of Peterson's store: David Sugar's General Merchandise store. Many accounts of Lake Villa's downtown during the turn of the century often conflict in part because of the high business turnover rate. (Courtesy of Tom and Sharon Barnstable.)

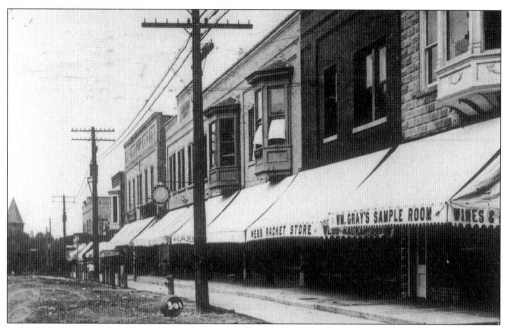

Lake Villa was not the only village in the area that exploded as a result of the train. Antioch, the village to the north of Lake Villa, developed a bustling business district in part because of the railroad. Unlike Lake Villa, however, Antioch was not created as a result of the railroad. Many early accounts of those living in Monaville and Angola refer to Antioch as a center for business.

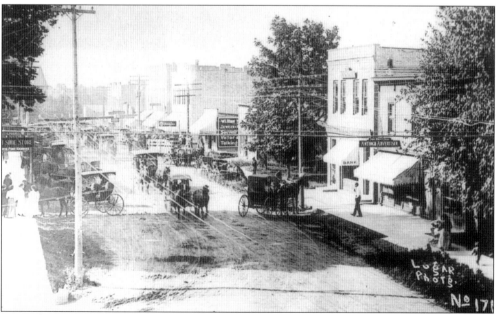

Antioch's prominence in the region continued throughout the last century. Even today, Lake Villa Township does not have its own high school; students either attend Antioch's to the north, or Grayslake's to the south. Lake Villa did, however, have the power to eventually break away from both townships, creating an independent government body. (Courtesy of Robert Frank and Infinity Web Designs.)

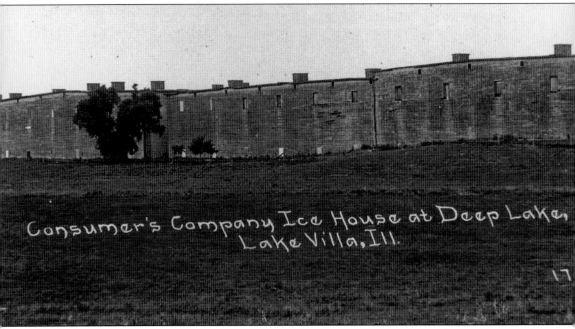

Consumer's Company Ice House at Deep Lake, Lake Villa, Ill.

Resorting was not the only major industry to infiltrate Lake Villa Township as a result of the railroad. A few years after the Wisconsin Central was opened, multiple icehouses such as the Consumer's Company Icehouse on Deep Lake were established. The ice industry's entrance to the region coincided with a growing commercial demand for thicker, cleaner ice than was typically harvested near Chicago. Particularly affecting the growth of this industry were the meatpacking plants of Chicago, which needed a way to keep meat from spoiling in railroad cars. In the winter of 1896, 40 railroad cars of ice were leaving Lake Villa daily; by 1906, this had expanded to 120 carloads a day.

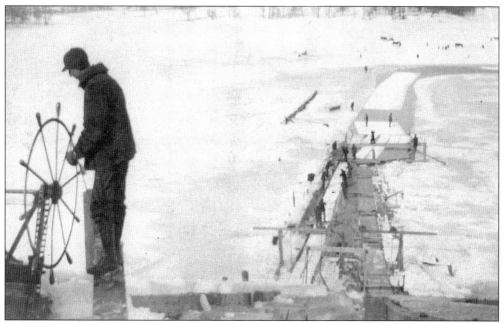

The ice-cutting industry did not only open up opportunities for local farmers looking for winter employment. Many migratory workers would often be brought in from Chicago to live and work at these icehouses as well. The Knickerbocker Icehouse, for example, had over 20 rooms set aside just to accommodate these transient workers. This photograph shows workers in Lake Villa harvesting ice.

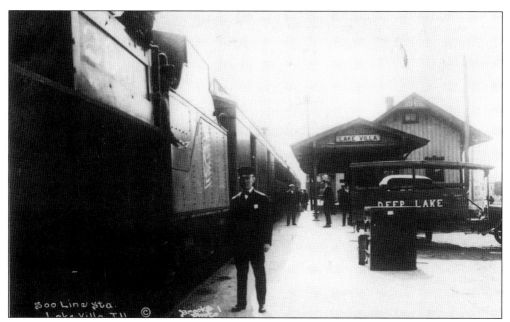

Many other industries grew out of the train's arrival to the region. Loon Lake, located between Antioch and Lake Villa, was the source of a dairy industry for many years. Harbaugh's lumber house also operated for many years with the help of the railroad. Even family resorts grew in stature. This photograph shows a taxi ready to take train passengers to Deep Lake's various resorts.

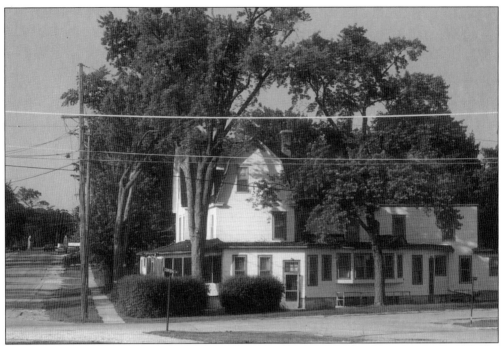

One of the few resorts left standing is the former Jarvis Hotel, located on the corner of Cedar and Central Avenues. Currently unoccupied, this structure has served various functions—nursing home, residence, and originally, another resort that appeared along side the railroad. (Photograph by author.)

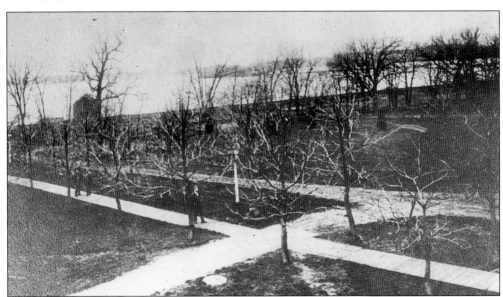

Strolling the lakeside grounds of the Lake Villa Hotel, an abundance of Chicago residents utilized the impressive railway network of the Windy City to find respite in the hinterland surrounding this urban center. Lake Villa Township was quite suitable to this goal if only because of its many lakes. E.J. Lehmann may have recognized this, and the result was one of the most impressive structures in all of Lake County.

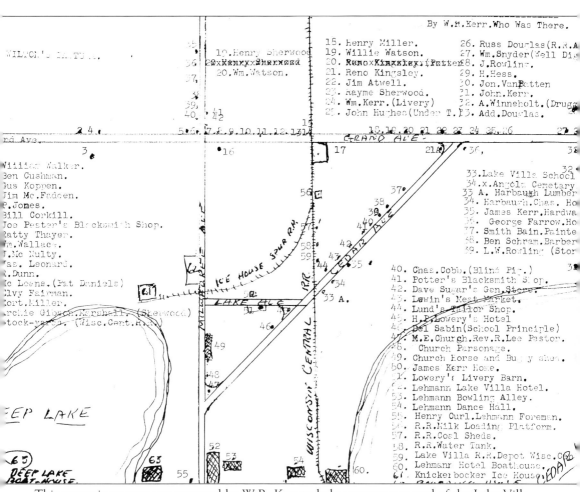

18. Henry Miller.
19. Willie Watson.
20. Reno Kingsley.(Potter)
21. Reno Kingsley.
22. Jim Atwell.
23. Rayme Sherwood.
24. Wm.Kerr.(Livery)
25. John Hughes(Under T.)

26. Russ Douglas(R.R.A
27. Wm.Snyder(Well Di
28. J.Rowling.
29. H.Hess.
30. Jon.VanPatten
31. John.Kerr.
32. A.Winneholt.(Drugg
33. Add.Douglas.

19.Henry Sherwood
20xKenyyxSherwood
20.Wm.Watson.

WILUCI.'U IM TU:.

GRAND AVE.

18.19.20 21 22 23 24 25.26

nd Ave.

William Walker.
Ben Cushman.
Gus Koppen.
Jim McFadden.
P.Jones.
Bill Corkill.
Joe Pester's Blacksmith Shop.
Patty Thayer.
Wm.Wallace.
J.McNulty.
Jas. Leonard.
A.Dunn.
Me Loans.(Pat Daniels)
Ilvy Fairman.
Cort.Miller.
Archie Giosch.Marshall (Sherwood)
Stock-yards. (Wisc.Cent.R.)

33.Lake Villa School
34.x.Angola Cemetary
33 A. Harbaugh Lumber
34. Harbaugh.Chas. Ho
35. James Kerr.Hardwa
36. George Farrow.Ho
37. Smith Bain.Painte
38. Ben Schram.Barber
39. L.W.Rowling (Stor

ICE HOUSE SPUR RR.

LAKE AVE

33 A.

40. Chas.Cobb.(Blind Pi:.)
41. Potter's Blacksmith Shop.
42. Dave Sugar's Gen.Store.
43. Lewin's Meat Market.
44. Lund's Tailor Shop.
45. H.P.Lowery's Hotel
46. Del Sabin(School Principle)
47. M.E.Church.Rev.R.Lee Pastor.
48. Church Parsonage.
49. Church Horse and Buggy shed.
50. James Kerr Home.
51. Lowery's Livery Barn.
52. Lehmann Lake Villa Hotel.
53. Lehmann Bowling Alley.
54. Lehmann Dance Hall.
55. Henry Curl.Lehmann Foreman.
56. R.R.Milk Loading Platform.
57. R.R.Coal Sheds.
58. R.R.Water Tank.
59. Lake Villa R.R.Depot Wisc.C
60. Lehmann Hotel Boathouse.
61. Knickerbocker Ice House.

WISCONSIN CENTRAL RR

CEDAR AVE

EP LAKE

DEEP LAKE
BOAT-HOUSE.

This typewritten map was prepared by W.R. Kerr to help preserve a record of the Lake Villa downtown triangle on the eve of its incorporation (1901). At its peak, Lake Villa's downtown boasted over 100 businesses, all serving the various needs of the nascent community. Regardless of Lehmann's original intentions, his decision to purchase a resort farm 50 miles north of Chicago marked the beginning of a new community where scattered farms existed just a decade before. By enticing the train, however, Lehmann also guaranteed that community a place of permanent significance within the network of the larger metropolitan area.

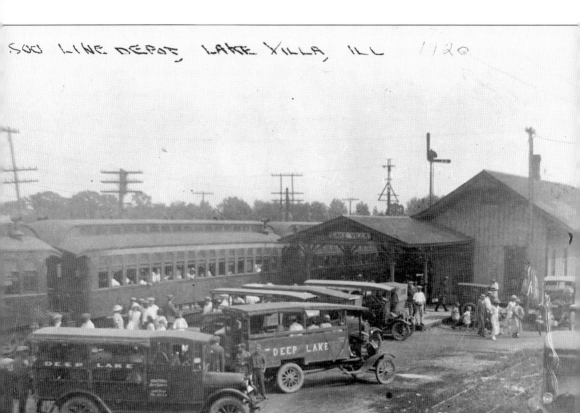

With an initial run of four daily passenger trains in 1886, by 1910, that number was over 14. Before the onset of a practical national road system, rail was the most effective way to escape the heat and crowds that typified summer in Chicago. Furthermore, for a growing American middle class, leisure and vacation time became reality for a wider segment of the population. The result for Lake Villa Township was the explosion of a new industry, and the weight of a new identity. An area once symbolized by farmers and blacksmiths, the new community of Lake Villa was best symbolized by resorts and rails. This identity would prove to be transient however. Within a few decades, a number of forces would conspire to transform the region's identity yet again.

Three

THE LEHMANNS

Yes I knew the Lehmanns. I worked in the grocery store. Yes, the town had very good relations with the Lehmanns. They were good, very down to earth people. . . . They gave people a lot of work [during the Depression].

—Marlene Coia

Lake Villa was very small, because the Lehmanns did not want to see this community grow. They came out here and settled, and they kept us small; there were all kinds of Lehmanns running around here.

—Dorothy Langbein

When Ernst J. Lehmann brought the train to Lake Villa Township, he left an indelible mark on the region. Nevertheless, Lehmann did manage to leave Lake Villa Township with a more lasting mark than even his grand resort—his family. Older residents remember the many estates and farms run by Lehmann's six children (a seventh, Charles, died as an infant). Edward John, Otto W., Ernst E., Emelie Wilhelmina, Augusta E., and Edith M. all held large stake in the community long after their father had passed on, and fondly or not, their legacy within the township remains.

For some, they were the wealthy benefactors of the township, softening the impact of both the economic woes of post-World War I America and the Great Depression. Not only did the Lehmann family control all of Cedar Lake, two-thirds of Deep Lake, and all of Sun Lake, but they also ran large gentleman farms, employing townspeople as servants and workers. During the Depression, this translated into job security for many residents.

Others believe the wealthy of the area did not often have the best interests of the townspeople involved. For most people, there is a general recognition that they controlled the village alongside a few select friends. Ed Gelden, longtime township resident, once articulated this story: "The northern area of Lake Villa was owned by the Lehmanns, the eastern end was owned by the Peacocks [Emelie Lehmann's husband was part of the famous jewelry family], and the southern portion was owned by the Sherwoods and the Wiltons."

Whether they were the saviors and benevolent patrons of a small town economy or the ruthless restrictors of progressive small business, Lehmann's six children seem to occupy the minds and memories of the older citizens of Lake Villa. Older residents share stories, anecdotes, and opinions on how the Lehmann dynasty related to the town of Lake Villa. Though it is difficult to ascertain what fragments of these stories are actually fact and which portions are now formalized myth, the very fact that the Lehmann dynasty has such a pervasive grasp on the consciousness of Lake Villa Township's elders is indicative of their importance in the township's history.

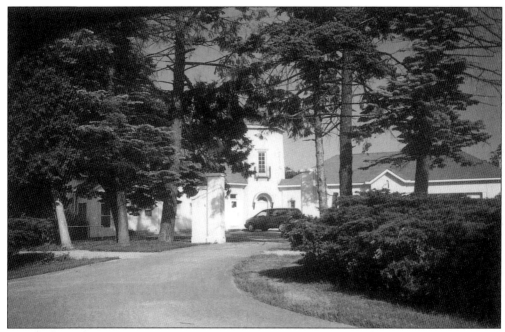

In 1888, Ernst J. Lehmann built a large stucco mansion on the western edge of Deep Lake. From his original purchase of 300 acres in 1883, Lehmann expanded his holdings to over 2,000 acres within Lake Villa Township in just five years. Lehmann's wife kept the house until 1918, when on her death it reverted to Augusta E., their daughter. Today the house and the surrounding grounds exist as a part of the Central Baptist Children's Home. (Photograph by author.)

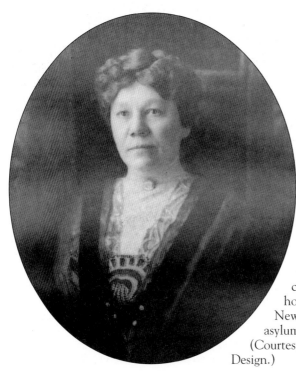

Though Augusta Lehmann, pictured here, married Ernst J. Lehmann in 1870–71, her loyalty to him may have been questionable. On April 19, 1890, Augusta was granted a court order placing Ernst into her custody. She had him committed to the Bloomingdale Asylum for the Insane in New York. Later, Lehmann was served with a summons that Augusta was applying for conservatorship of his $2.5 million holdings while he waited for the train to New York. By the time he had reached the asylum, a judge had granted her application. (Courtesy of Robert Frank and Infinity Web Design.)

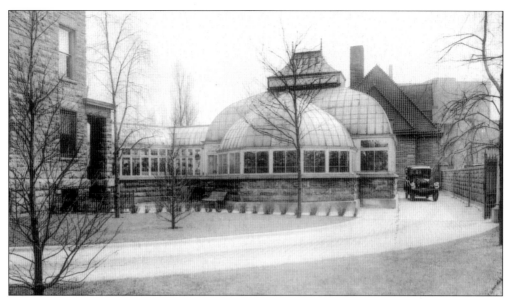

With E.J. Lehmann gone, Edward John took on many of his father's responsibilities. By 1905, Edward was president of the now enormous Fair Store, and as E.J. Lehmann's oldest son, he became the manager of the Lehmann estate. This photograph of Edward's Chicago townhome reflects the level of wealth the Lehmann family had amassed by the turn of the century. This particular view offers a glimpse of the greenhouse and atrium facility on the premises. (Courtesy of Robert Frank and Infinity Web Design.)

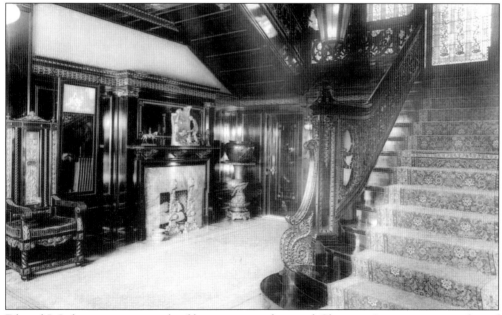

Edward J. Lehmann spent much of his time in and around Chicago. A prominent member of elite organizations such as the Chicago Athletic Club, South Shore Country Club, Edgewater Golf Club, and the Congressional Club of Washington D.C., Edward prided himself on both his firm business hand and his ability to live well. This photograph reveals the ornate staircase found in Edward's Chicago townhome. (Courtesy of Robert Frank and Infinity Web Design.)

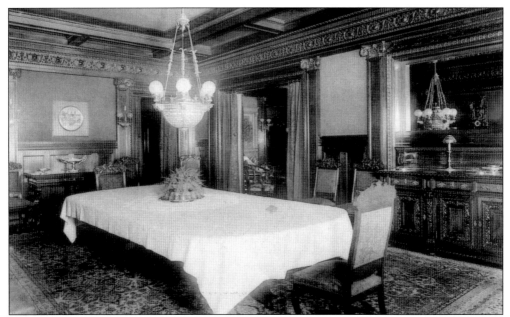

The dining room of Edward's townhome was just as ornate as the rest of the house, full of mirrors and heavy ornamentation. The Lehmann children lived lavishly from their father's estate, though each pursued individual manifestations of wealth. One possible address for this townhome is 3662 Sheridan Road (Lake Shore Drive). If the address is in fact accurate, then the site of Edward's magnificent home is currently a high-rise apartment complex. (Courtesy of Robert Frank and Infinity Web Design.)

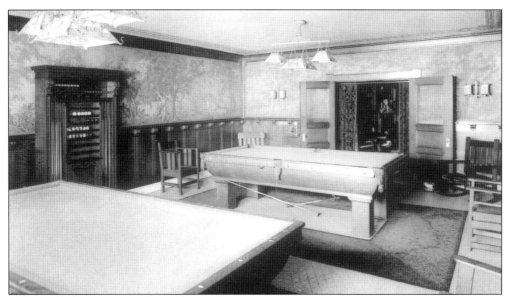

Gaming was another important aspect of the Lehmann family. The Lake Villa Hotel's island casino clubhouse operated long after Ernst had passed away. Some anecdotes relay that the clubhouse actually operated as a speakeasy during the Prohibition years, though there is strong evidence that the casino was gone by 1920. This photograph displays the billiard room of Edward's townhome. (Courtesy of Robert Frank and Infinity Web Design.)

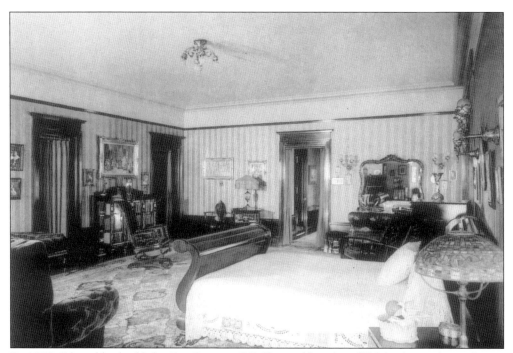

By 1925, Edward had sold the Fair Store to S.S. Kresge (founder of K-Mart) in order to devote his time fully to the management of the Lehmann estate. Never again would a member of the Lehmann family have a stake in the grand department store that had made them wealthy. (Courtesy of Robert Frank and Infinity Web Design.)

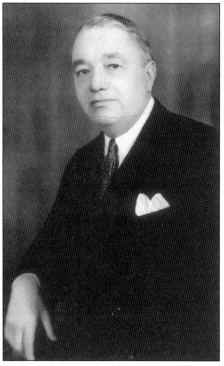

Edward John Lehmann was known as an austere man by many of his contemporaries. Aside from bearing the heavy responsibilities of presiding over the Fair Store and the Lehmann estate, however, Edward also pursued many personal passions in his spare time. Edward pursued these passions at Longwood Farm, located in Lake Villa just north of his father's former estate. (Courtesy of Robert Frank and Infinity Web Design.)

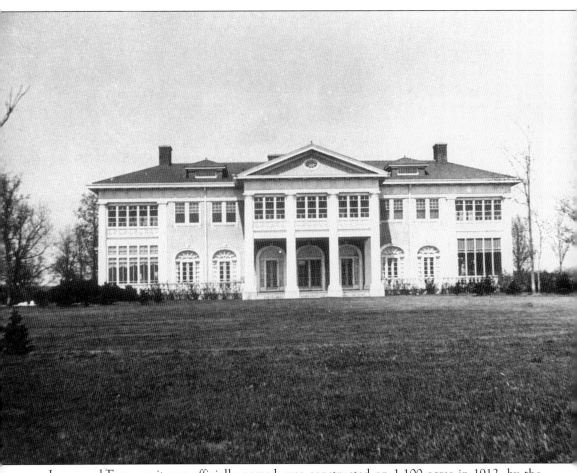

Longwood Farm, as it was officially named, was constructed on 1,100 acres in 1912, by the Hamlin brothers as a summer home for Edward J. Lehmann and his family. Edward often referred to the opulent estate as "the cottage." Every room connects to a porch or verandah, and a ballroom was added in 1927. At its peak, this estate included a half-mile equestrian racetrack, a nine-hole golf course, pool, greenhouse, a private lake (Sun Lake), and cottages to house over 100 servants and employees. Breeding top show horses was one of Edward's favorite pastimes during his summers in Lake Villa Township. (Courtesy of Robert Frank and Infinity Web Design.)

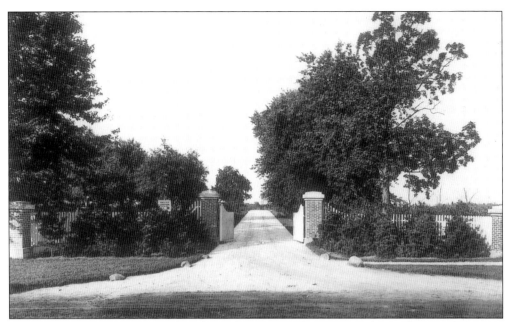

Even on vacation, however, Edward J. Lehmann was known as a demanding employer. For example, Longwood Farm had one servant whose sole task was raking horseshoe prints off of the crushed limestone driveway pictured here. According to Irv Buchta, whose family lived on the farm for over 30 years, Mr. Lehmann once chased him down and grabbed him when he was a young boy, threatening that he should never ride his pony across the driveway. (Courtesy of Robert Frank and Infinity Web Design.)

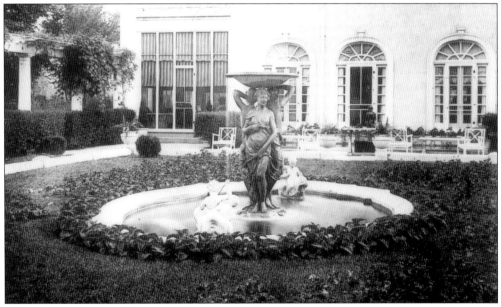

Though many of the trappings of rural life could be found at Longwood Farm, the large estate also contained the style of a wealthy merchant prince. This picture of the courtyard behind the farm is a testament to the wealth and elegance that could be afforded by the Lehmann family, even during the height of the Great Depression. (Courtesy of Robert Frank and Infinity Web Design.)

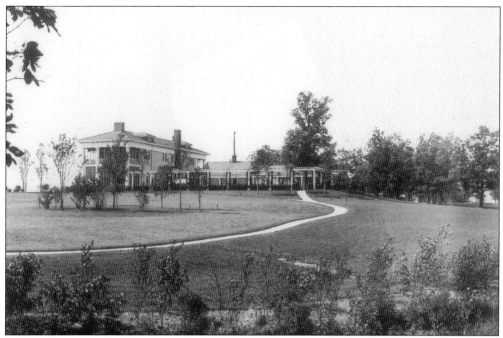

By many accounts, the Lehmann family helped many local township residents through the Great Depression. For example, Edward J. hired many caddies from the village during this time, giving them "big money" for the early 1930s. Dorothy Langbein recounts her experience as a caddie: "I used to caddie for them when I was younger. They had that little golf course behind Longwood Farm, and they would take us back to the big house, treat us royally, and then their chauffeur would take us home." (Courtesy of Robert Frank and Infinity Web Design.)

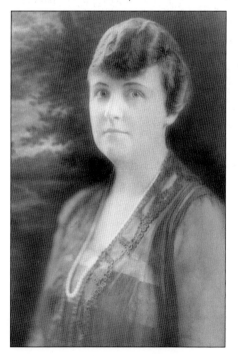

Florence Lehmann was Edward John's second wife. After Edward J. died in 1954, Florence was pressured to sell Longwood Farm, long considered a financial drain. Florence, however, refused to sell her beloved rural estate. At her death in 1964, Longwood Farm was finally auctioned off, but her tenacity has made this estate the only remaining Lehmann property still extant, excluding those converted for a new purpose. (Courtesy of Robert Frank and Infinity Web Design.)

50

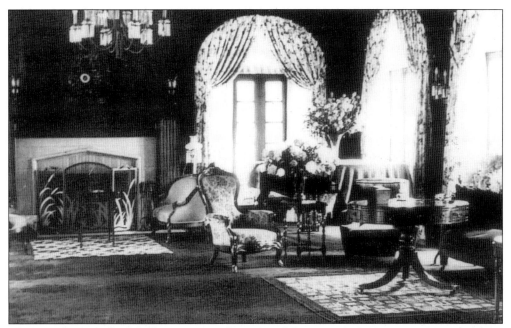

This is a photograph of the living room of Longwood Farm, c. 1940. Even summers were spent in luxury on the estate. Note the swamp reeds and cattails on the fireplace grill; they were designed to evoke the landscape of Sun Lake, once part of the estate's acreage. (Courtesy of Robert Frank and Infinity Web Design.)

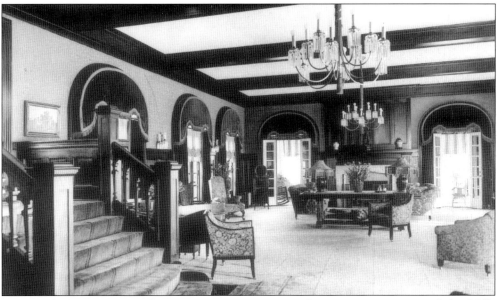

Longwood Farm's present-day existence is a source of some controversy in Lake Villa Township. For some local residents, Lehmann Mansion (as it is popularly referred to today) is seen as the number-one candidate for historical renovation. For others, however, the expensive nature of any serious renovation attempt on the mansion is seen as a major detraction. Only time will tell if the now worn mansion survives into the next decade. (Courtesy of Robert Frank and Infinity Web Design.)

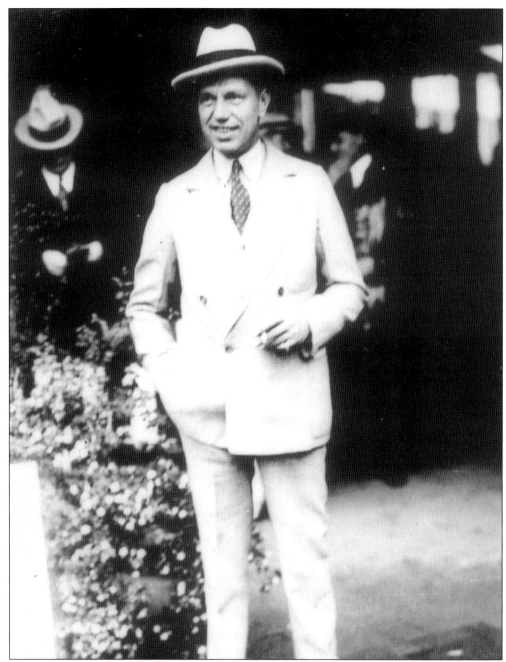

Though Edward J. Lehmann was often seen as the de facto head of the Lehmann estate, he was by no means the only Lehmann active within the township. Otto W. Lehmann, pictured here, was known as the festive and wild brother, and the prankster of the family. Unlike his brother Edward J., Otto had little to do with running the financial affairs of his father, seeming more content to spend the money than to worry over it. Common knowledge has it that he frequented both Wolff's Resort and the Green Mill, local bars in the area. Of all the Lehmanns, Otto was often considered to have the most social contact with the township's "common" folk. (Courtesy of Robert Frank and Infinity Web Design.)

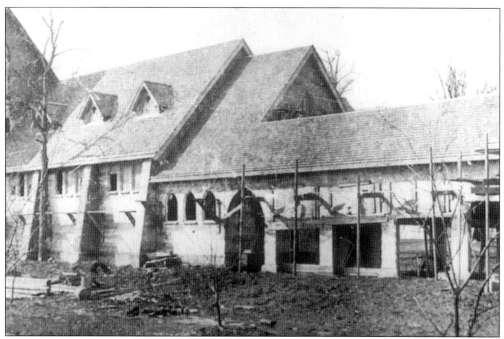

Otto's estate, Chesney Farms, was located on 600 acres overlooking Columbia Bay on the western edge of Lake Villa Township. Like the rest of the Lehmann family, Otto's summer residence was just as lavish. This photograph of Chesney Farm's construction reveals the immense proportions of Otto's estate. (Courtesy of Robert Frank and Infinity Web Design.)

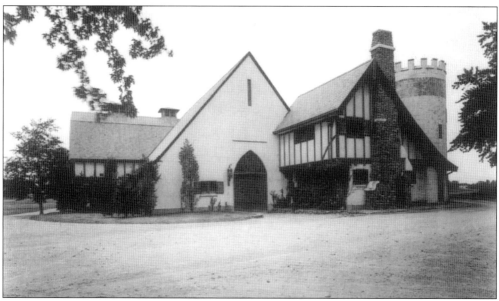

Otto's wild behavior did have interesting results at times. For example, Otto's first marriage was to a Ms. Affeld, the ex-wife of his brother, Ernst E. Lehmann. In 1927, Otto had a boxing ring constructed in his barn exclusively for the practice of Gene Tunney, who used the space to prepare for a rematch against boxing great Jack Dempsey. This photograph shows the finished look of the grand Chesney Farms. (Courtesy of Robert Frank and Infinity Web Design.)

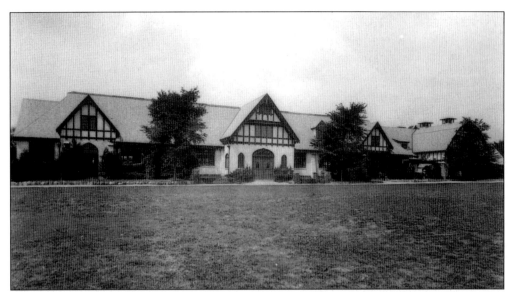

In 1954, a year after Otto's death, the acreage of his estate in combination with former Chicago mayor Fred Busse's farm to the south was broken into a residential subdivision today known as Chesney Shores and Fox Lake Hills. The estate itself remains to this day, though now it is known as the Church of the Holy Family. (Courtesy of Robert Frank and Infinity Web Design)

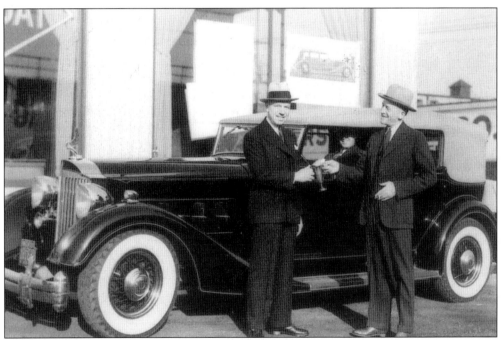

Otto generated a few unforgettable moments among local township residents. For instance, Otto is rumored to have faked his death on at least one occasion. Another incident, remembered well by a few older people, was the time he threatened to burn a whole bar down when the proprietor refused to sell cigarettes to some recently returned World War II veterans. Otto is pictured here getting a brand new 1935 Packard. (Courtesy of Robert Frank and Infinity Web Design.)

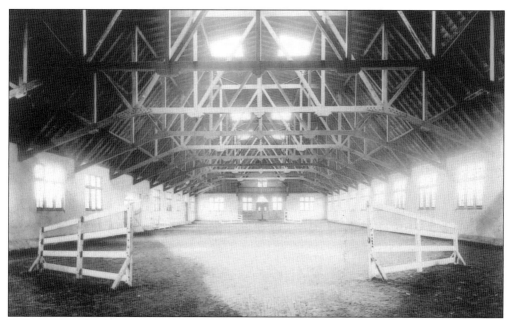

Different from his brother Edward J. in a variety of ways, Otto did, however, share his passion for breeding and riding top horses. The pictured riding arena was part of Otto's immense barn, which had 24 separate stalls for prize-winning Arabian horses. Otto was also the president of the Arlington Jockey Club for a brief period. (Courtesy of Robert Frank and Infinity Web Design.)

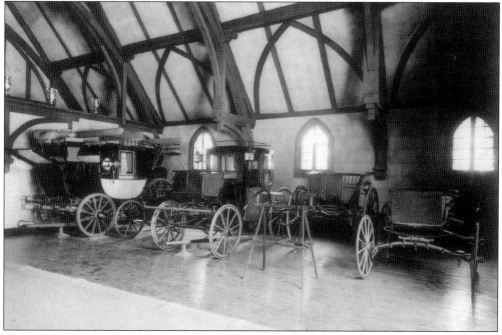

The Chesney Farms barn was quite a complex in its own right. In addition to the aforementioned features, this facility also had an area to house Otto's many buggies. Otto often used this transportation to get in and around the largely rural township. (Courtesy of Robert Frank and Infinity Web Design.)

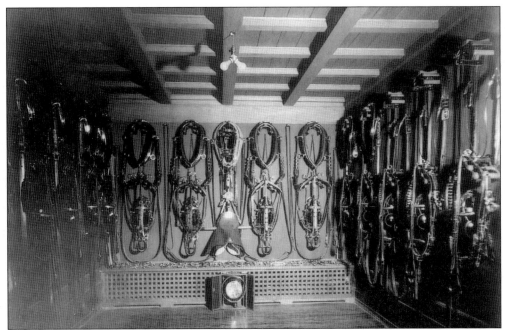

The many bridles pictured above were for use with Otto's Arabian horses. The affinity for equestrian hobbies shared by many in the Lehmann family seems to have contributed to their continued presence in the township well after their parents' passing. Even the Lehmann sisters were known for holding opulent horse shows on the grounds of the present day Lake Villa Post Office. (Courtesy of Robert Frank and Infinity Web Design.)

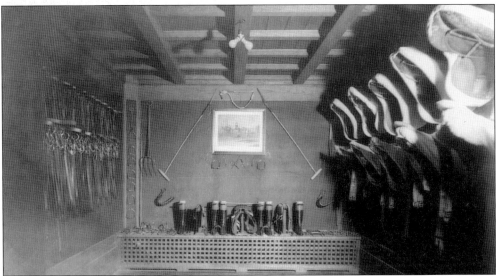

An equestrian estate did leave time for more than just breeding and showing horses as this polo equipment attests. Overall, the influence of Ernst J. Lehmann's children in Lake Villa Township (c. 1900–1950) is typically underestimated. While the dramatic physical and structural effects that the elder Lehmann had on Lake Villa during the 19th century are well chronicled, the profound social, political, and economic influence of his children are just as important, if not more so. (Courtesy of Robert Frank and Infinity Web Design.)

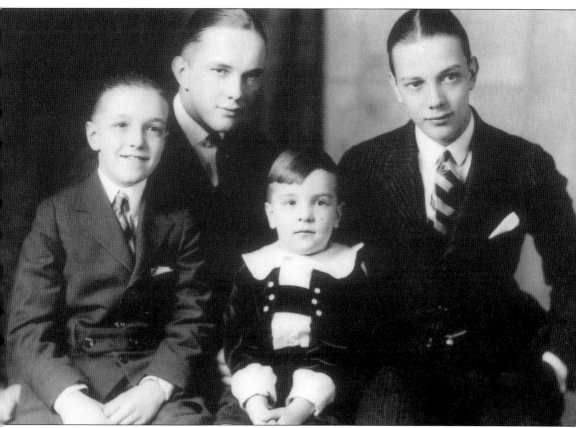

After nearly 70 years of influence in the Lake Villa Township area, the Lehmann family had all but disappeared by the end of the 1950s. As the children of Ernst J. Lehmann passed on, early death and lack of interest pushed most of the family away from the area. In the photograph above, Edward J.'s four surviving children are pictured from left to right: George W., Ernst J., Robert O., and Edward J. Jr. Tragically, early death took George (42), Ernst (36), and Edward (41). Today, the pervasive influence of the Lehmann family can only be found in the many mansions, stories, and in the railroads presence. (Courtesy of Robert Frank and Infinity Web Design.)

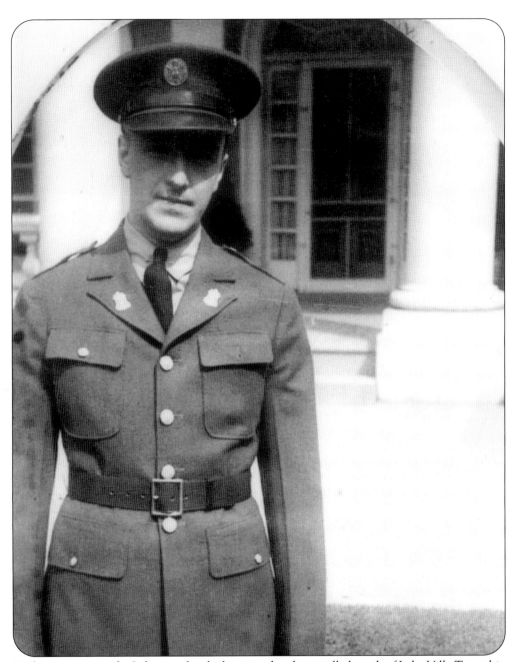

For better or worse, the Lehmann family dominated and controlled much of Lake Villa Township throughout the first half of the 20th century. From politics to personal lives, the wealth and lifestyle of this family has provided the fodder for many memories and stories. The Lehmann's largesse as well as their unchecked power within the community is a topic of heated debate and further research, much like that currently being undertaken by Lehmann scholar, Candace Saunders. There is, however, a very human side to this larger than life family. For example, George Lehmann (shown here in uniform), son of Edward J., served bravely in World War II. It is this humanity, after all, that makes the more extraordinary qualities of the Lehmann family so fascinating in the first place. (Courtesy of Robert Frank and Infinity Web Design.)

Four
AFTER THE BOOM

My opinion on the development in the area? I get a little upset with it, because for me, I love the small town. For a kid growing up it was great.

—Marlene Coia

For all of Lake Villa Township's potential as a vacation haven, the village could not sustain the rapid residential and commercial growth of the first decades of the 20th century. Events such as World War I, subsequent national economic crises and panics, and the shifting industry needs of Chicago all contributed to the region's commercial undoing. It was the beginning of the end for E.J. Lehmann's dream. The next 25 years would leave Lake Villa Township all but forgotten by the mighty Chicago.

In the two decades after the Lake Villa Hotel burned, the village's primary industry, resorting, began a precipitous drop. One indicator of this change: passenger trains. Throughout the 1920s, the number of passenger trains through the Village of Lake Villa continually declined. By 1932, only 8 trains were making daily passenger stops as compared to 14 in 1910. By the end of the decade, that number had dwindled to 4. During this same time, the housing for railroad employees that had been constructed at the beginning of the century was razed. The railroad was no longer the heart of the village, the resorts no longer its limbs.

Resorting was not the only industry affected. Other industries important to Lake Villa Township also declined during this period. According to many sources, the winter of 1915 witnessed the closure of the Knickerbocker Icehouse. The structure was razed in March of 1915, and the railroad spur that connected the southern shore of Deep Lake to the rail line was removed. The ice-cutting industry was no longer profitable with the advent of modern refrigeration. With the disappearance of the icehouse, many seasonal migrant workers had no reason to return. The milk trains stopped running some time between 1922 and 1928, marking the end of another prominent railroad industry.

As industry declined, growth in the township began to stabilize. With this stability, the Village of Lake Villa, the crown jewel of western Lake County, transformed into a sleepy exurban village.

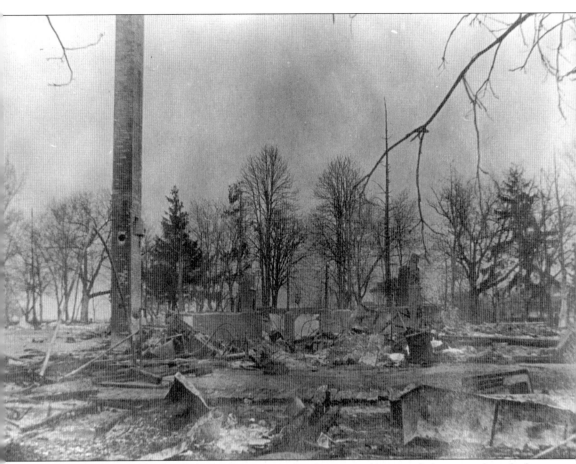

After the first decade of the 20th century, the fervent resort crowds began a slow decline. Specific events during the 1910s foreshadowed this change in Lake Villa's economic and social construction. On the night of April 16, 1914, the grand Lake Villa Hotel, symbol of Ernst J. Lehmann's influence on the town, burned in a spectacle that could purportedly be seen from Waukegan, nearly 13 miles away. While day tripping remained a cornerstone of Lake Villa business for several years after, no attempts were made to rebuild the hotel, and the resort industry in the village began to disappear.

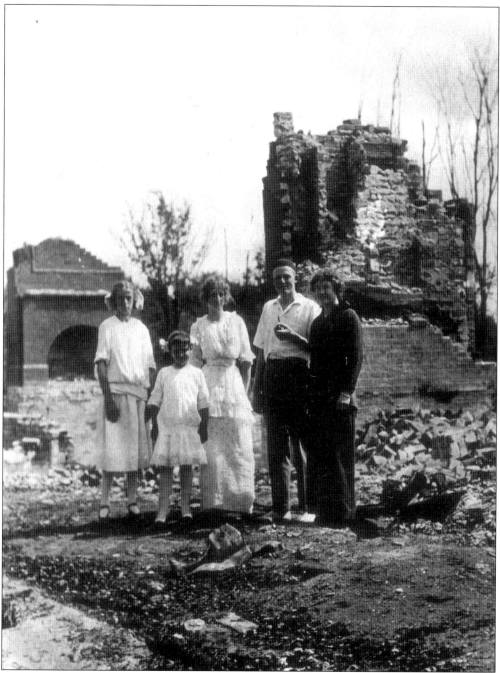

The sight of the charred Lake Villa Hotel not only drew headlines but curious visitors as well. The once mighty resort complex was gone in a matter of hours. Other resorts remained in business (a handful still exist today) long after the tragic fire, but in the end, none could match the appeal or commercial power of the Lake Villa Hotel. In this particular photograph, the following people came to examine the two fireplaces of what was once the hotel's lobby: (from supposed left to right) Ruby Falch, Elizabeth Jarvis, Stella (Helen) Kerr, Ray Kerr, and Helen (Stella) Kerr. (Courtesy of Bill and Carol Effinger.)

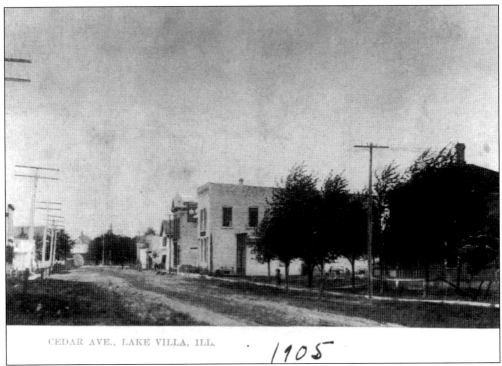

CEDAR AVE., LAKE VILLA, ILL.   1905

This 1905 postcard reveals an atypically serene day on Cedar Avenue. As decades passed, this downtown would grow in prominence as the resorts along Route 83 slowly disappeared. Nonetheless, the Village of Lake Villa as a whole began to slow in pace and activity. (Courtesy of Bill and Carol Effinger.)

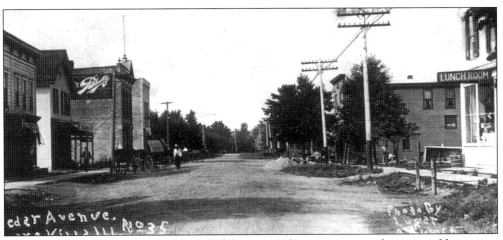

Though Cedar Avenue became Lake Villa's primary business center, the types of businesses began transforming from regional or resort-driven businesses to those more local in nature, such as the Lunch Room, pictured on the right. (Courtesy of Bill and Carol Effinger.)

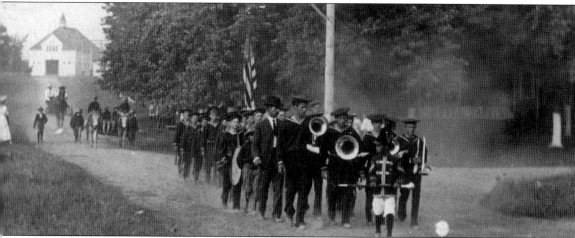

Other major institutions also called Lake Villa home. Captain Edward Lounsberry Bradley founded Allendale, a home and school for orphaned or troubled boys on the western shore of Cedar Lake in 1897. Originally serving six young boys with only $25 in his pocket, Allendale is still in operation today, having served thousands of boys and girls in need of a variety of assistance. This photograph pictures the Allendale Boys Band marching on Cedar Avenue away from Route 83. Playing for a Fourth of July celebration in 1907, the band is passing the Hotel Jarvis, pictured to the right. Captain Bradley is on the left side of the band in a derby hat and suit. Also notable in this photograph is the enormous John Stratton bus barn standing atop the hill in the background. (Courtesy of Bill and Carol Effinger.)

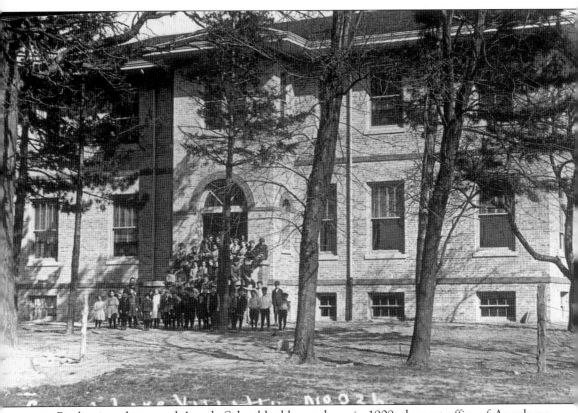

By the time the second Angola School had burnt down in 1909, the post office of Angola no longer existed. Lake Villa was the only incorporated village within the township limits, so the construction of a third school was moved to the northwestern corner of Route 132 and 83. The site of the old Sherwood home, this third school was two stories high and made of all brick. When school began again during the 1909 school year, L.W. Felker retained the position of principal. With many additions, this school is still used today, under the name Joseph J. Pleviak School. The part of the school pictured here was replaced as late as 1979. (Courtesy of Bill and Carol Effinger.)

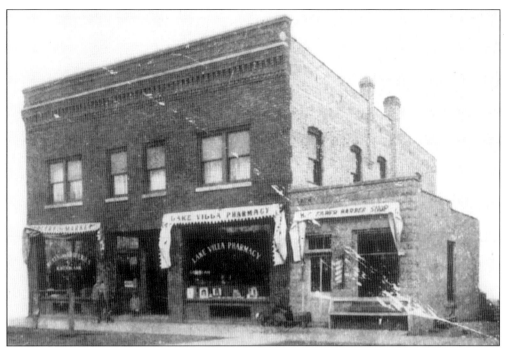

The Lake Villa Pharmacy, pictured here in 1913, was one of the most prominent stores on all of Cedar Avenue. For many years, this store was run by Bert J. Hooper, a strong civic leader in the area who fought for the interests of Lake Villa's "common" residents.

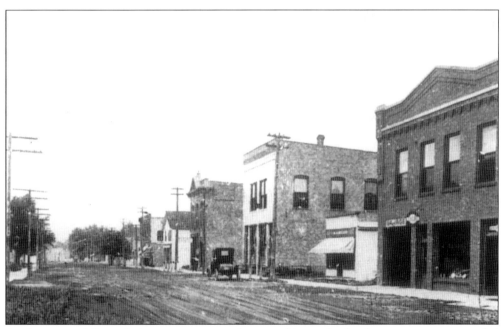

As the automobile made its appearance on the township roads, the downtown area responded by adding such stores as the repair garage seen on the right. A little later, the Hucker family brought a Chrysler dealership to Cedar Avenue, giving the automobile a permanent place in the heart of Lake Villa's business district.

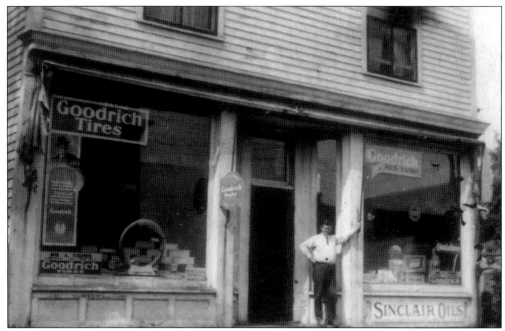

Originally located on the west side of Cedar Avenue, Effinger's Hardware is the longest family-owned business in the whole township. Opened in 1923 by John Effinger and his wife, Ada, the business was then passed to Bill and Carol Effinger, and then again to Mike Effinger, who runs the store today. (Courtesy of Tom and Sharon Barnstable.)

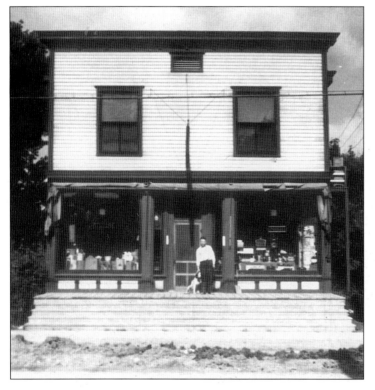

Though Effinger's Hardware is still open for business, it is now located on Grand Avenue across from McKinley Avenue. This store is symbolic of the stability and tradition that settled over Lake Villa following the departure of the major resort complexes. In many respects, the village prided itself on continuity and dependability, two things exemplified by many of the businesses and families in the area. (Courtesy of Bill and Carol Effinger.)

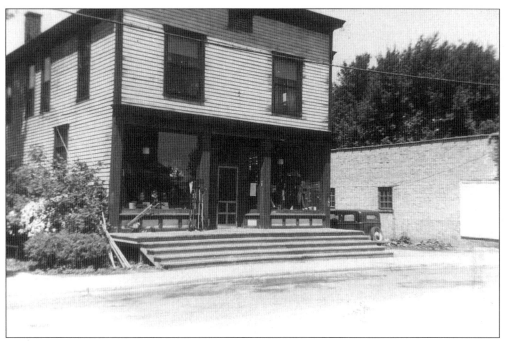

Though the great resorts from the turn of the century had gone, the many beautiful lakes of the area still drew crowds to the township on the weekends and in summer months. Fishing remained one of the biggest draws of the area, as demonstrated by the stack of large rod fishing poles for sale just to the left of Effinger's Hardware store. (Courtesy of Bill and Carol Effinger.)

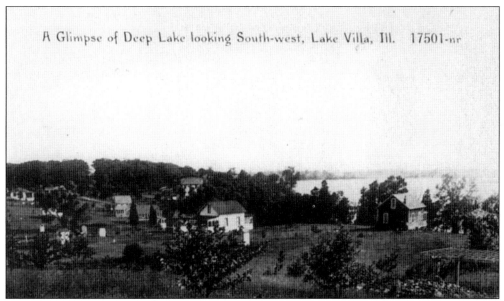

A Glimpse of Deep Lake looking South-west, Lake Villa, Ill. 17501-nr

During this period, the construction of residential homes outside of Lake Villa's downtown area began to increase. This photograph shows the development of small homes and farms on the northeastern shore of Deep Lake. Many families that had vacationed in Lake Villa Township during the turn of the century were now purchasing permanent homes in the area, one manifestation of America's rapid suburban development.

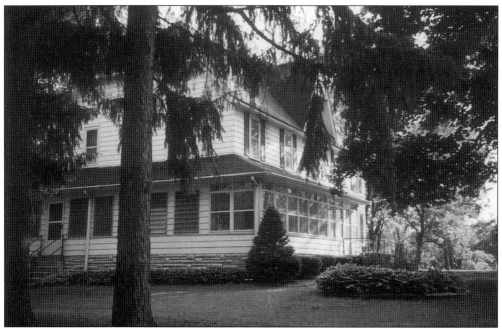

One long-standing institution within the heart of Lake Villa is the Danube-Swabian German Aid Society. Founded in 1925, the society has given help to a variety of causes and continues humanitarian work from its Lake Villa facility. The Aid Society is located just west of the downtown triangle on Route 132. (Photograph by author.)

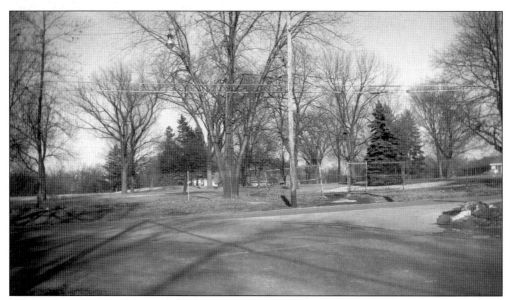

After Lake Villa Hotel burned down, many ancillary industries closed down. This photograph shows the now vacant intersection of Route 83 and Cedar Avenue, once the home to the immense Lake Villa Hotel Stable and Bus Barn. John Stratton, principal owner of the bus barn, eventually became the first township supervisor of Lake Villa Township when it was created in 1913.

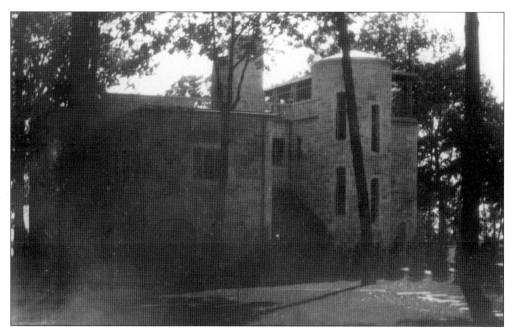

The Lehmann children were not the only proprietors of large estates in the township area. Other wealthy families in the area included the Peacock family, the Haerther family, as well as the Willet family. This photograph depicts the mansion of the Willet family, located on Dering Street on the western end of Lake Villa Township. (Courtesy Tom and Sharon Barnstable.)

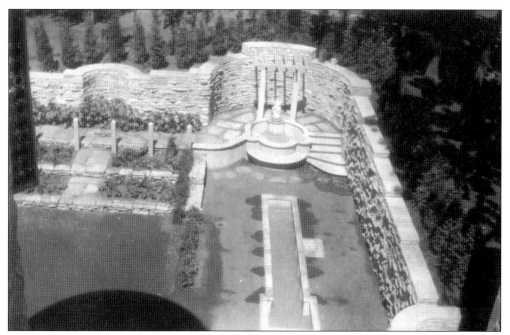

The Willet family fortune grew from the Willet Bus Company, a highly successful transportation firm. This photograph reveals the impressive and imposing courtyard of the Willet mansion. Estates such as these mixed rural elements and rustic charm with ostentatious displays of wealth. (Courtesy of Tom and Sharon Barnstable.)

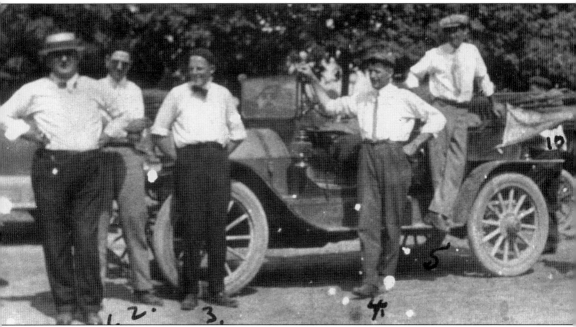

Though the elite of Lake Villa Township created a particular fascination among people, the vast majority of residents in the region were by no means wealthy. Nevertheless, though many local families had little money or property, the community of Lake Villa was tight-knit. In many ways, the pioneer spirit of the early township post offices manifested itself in new ways among Lake Villa residents. This photograph chronicles an automobile trip from Lake Villa to Lake Geneva made in 1910. Most of the men on this trip were local civic leaders of the time. Pictured from left to right are: Charley Keller, Norm Leutener, Ray Kerr, Frank Hamlin, Fred Bartlell, and George Mitchell (obscured by car rear). (Courtesy of Bill and Carol Effinger.)

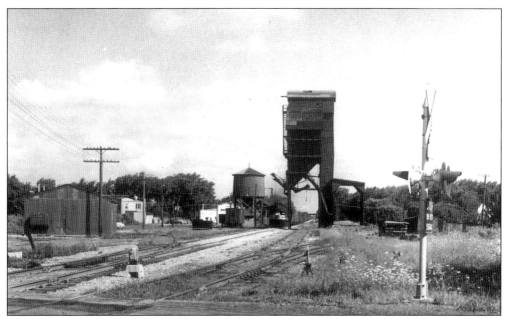

Soon after the resorting industry began its steady decline, other railroad-based local industries followed suit. After the ice and milk trains ceased and lumber trains grew more infrequent, only a few remnants of past industry remained untouched. One such remnant was the great coal dock, which operated from 1928 to 1956, dispensing coal to passing trains. Like other sections of the Lake Villa rail yard, the coal dock was eventually razed.

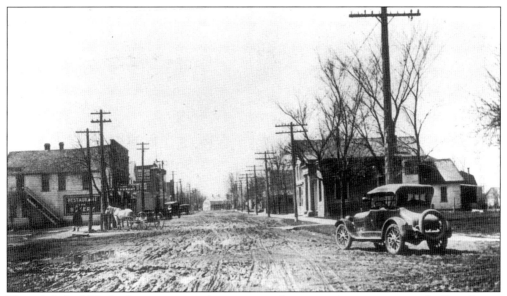

Though Lake Villa had in many ways become a modern town, certain aspects of village living hearkened back to the days before the railroad. One example is the poor condition of the roads throughout Lake Villa Township. From Monaville Road on the township's southern edge to Town Line Road in the north, just a little rain made many local roads quickly impassable. This poor road quality was even evident in the heart of Lake Villa's downtown as this photograph suggests.

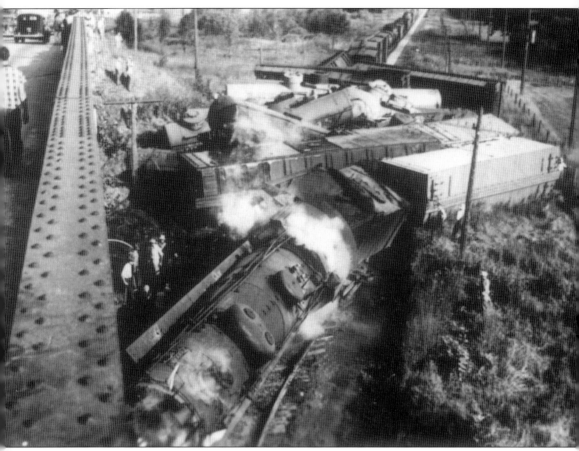

On August 30, 1939, 19 cars derailed on an eastbound freight train going through Lake Villa. Eventually, it was discovered that sabotage was the cause of the accident, perpetrated by mentally unstable Wisconsin resident John Bourne. Though no one was killed, the tampered track switch, which caused the accident, would have derailed a crowded passenger train due through Lake Villa about 20 minutes after the accident. Of larger concern to working crews, however, was the dangerous automobile traffic conditions created on Route 83 by curious bystanders observing the train wreck. John Bourne was eventually found insane and sentenced to psychiatric treatment and hospitalization.

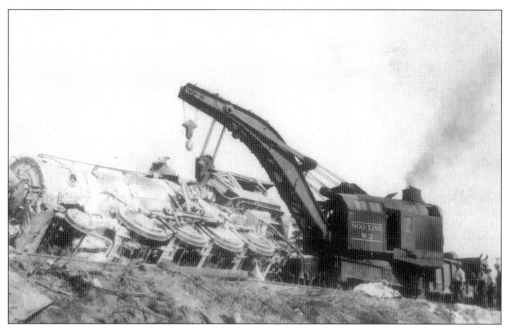

Though no one was hurt, the train wreck created a difficult clean-up task for all those involved. The Soo Line even used a crane to lift and move the extremely heavy engine and boxcars. Some of the local residents who helped in the clean-up effort were: Carl Bock, Charlie Hamlin, Frank Slazes, Frank Sciacero, and Joe Dada. (Courtesy of Tom and Sharon Barnstable.)

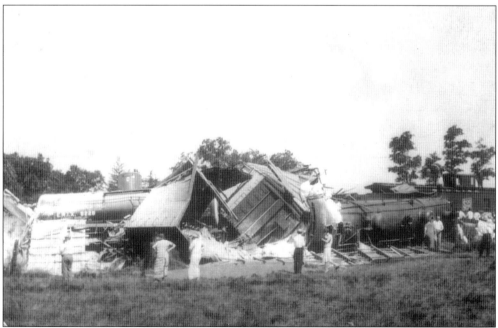

In a railroad town, incidents like the August 1939 train wreck are to be expected. There have been other instances of train wrecks in Lake Villa, such as the 1968 wreck pictured here. Derailed remnants for this particular wreck remained in the area for many years after the event. (Tom and Sharon Barnstable.)

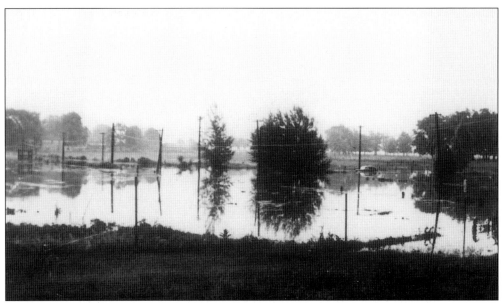

Despite all the advances made by the Village of Lake Villa in the first few decades of the 20th century, many forces of nature cannot be conquered. For instance, the frequent flooding that occurs in the low-lying areas throughout the township will always be an issue, particularly in certain sections of Petite Lake Road and Route 132 west of Fairfield Road. These problems still plague the township today.

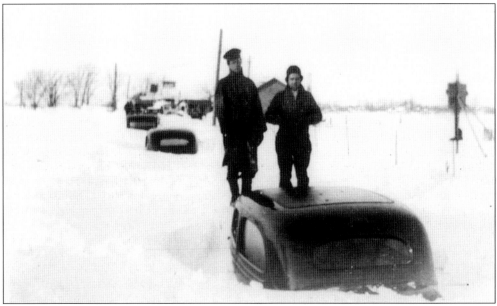

Every season brings its natural hazards, including the winter months. In this photo (left to right), Bill Oldstone and Howard Wilton stand on the roof of a car to show the depth of the "big snow" of 1935. All cars in this photograph run along the Route 83, just south of Route 132. The Village of Lake Villa, with or without a bustling resort industry, was the indisputable center of Lake Villa Township. As the Great Depression began to wane, however, the long subjugated unincorporated hamlets of the township would begin to shine in their own right.

74

Five

HAMLETS

Lake Villa didn't always want to see [Venetian Village and West Miltmore] grow, but eventually we put enough of our people in the government, and then they started listening.

—Patricia Tranberg

As the Village of Lake Villa rapidly grew and developed, other sections of the larger Lake Villa Township became easily forgotten. Nevertheless, the unincorporated hamlets (as they are sometimes called) that make up the balance of the township (Venetian Village, West Miltmore, Third Lake, and for a time, the Monaville area) have played a vital role in the progress of the region. These hamlets have contained resorts, industry, and important local families as well. In fact, the history of the Village of Lake Villa is so inextricably linked to the history of the various township hamlets, that to ignore their unique history is to rob Lake Villa of its broader context.

While Monaville had been a significant post in the township for the earliest European settlers, Venetian Village was the first formal hamlet of the township (the community of Monaville has since been completely annexed into the Village of Lake Villa). As Venetian Village expanded, however, the area split and West Miltmore became its own hamlet. Third Lake, meanwhile, is a small, unincorporated enclave on the eastern edge of the township. The old post office of Sand Lake, primarily Ernst E. Lehmann's Lindenhurst farm by the 1920s, was also an unincorporated area for a time. Together, these areas represent the complete fabric of Lake Villa Township.

Unfortunately, the history of these areas is obscured by lack of records, political documents, etc. . . . . For the history of these places, oral history is the most reliable and ready source. These hamlets have just as many wonderful stories to give, if one is willing to listen.

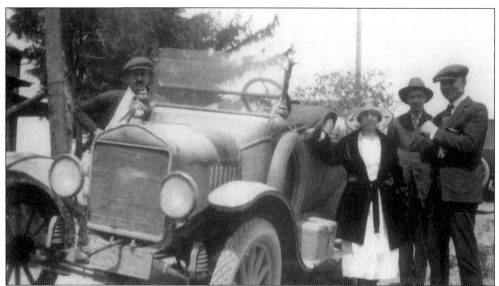

After the turn of the century, Monaville industry rapidly declined. Many of the original families from the area, however, remained in Monaville, taking care of the East Fox Lake Cemetery and other remnants of the trading post's past. Pictured here are Monaville residents going to pay their respects at the East Fox Lake Cemetery. The reason for this trip is most likely Memorial Day, as this trip took place on May 30, 1920. (Courtesy of Tom and Sharon Barnstable.)

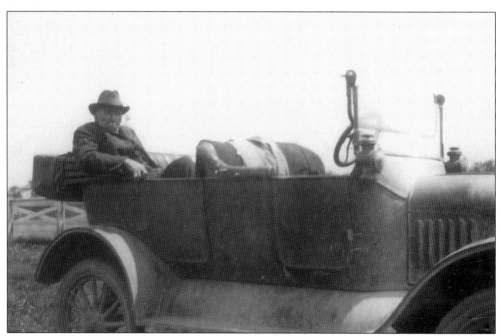

This photograph is from the same trip, but the man in the photograph is the elderly Robert Tweed. One of the proprietors of the Monaville Tweed store, he would have remembered the trading post in its heyday before the railroad. (Courtesy of Tom and Sharon Barnstable.)

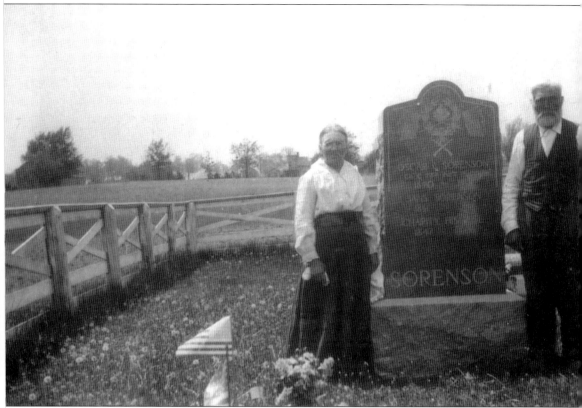

This photograph is also from the Memorial Day trip. Inside of East Fox Lake Cemetery, Jans and his wife Charity Sorenson (previously pictured as "Gramma" in Chapter 1) stand beside the grave of their son Oscar Sorenson. Oscar was killed while serving in the military during World War I. At the time of this photograph, Oscar would have only been deceased for approximately two years. The East Fox Lake Cemetery is more than a testament to the hundreds of individuals interred there; it is a testament to a lost community, to the people who were forgotten by the train. (Courtesy of Tom and Sharon Barnstable.)

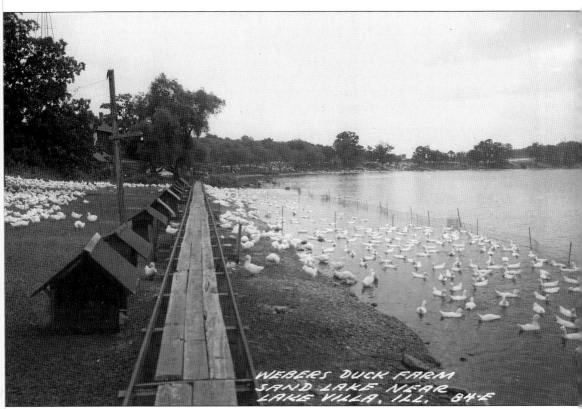

Lake Villa was not the only source of industry in the township either. Farms and resorts throughout the region contributed to the township's overall economic health. One large industry located on Sand Lake and Slough Lake was the Weber Duck Farm. Many residents remember the duck farm mostly by the smells it created at different times of the year. Other local residents, however, worked on the duck farm at one time or another. Former duck pickers include Gordon Martin, Bob Tanner, Hank Jarvis, and Fred Nielsen. These workers typically received 7¢ per duck through the 1940s and 1950s.

In addition to residential and commercial construction, the various hamlets of Lake Villa Township also included public institutions such as schools. Sand Lake School District 48 served those students at the eastern end of the township. Shown here before its renovation in the 1930s, Sand Lake School District 48 served students until March 14, 1947, when it was annexed into the Lake Villa School District. By 1952, the schoolhouse was sold to private owners.

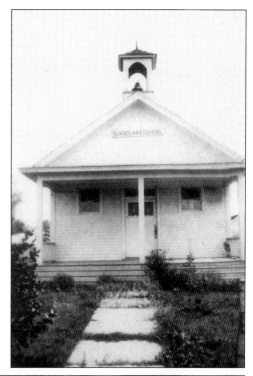

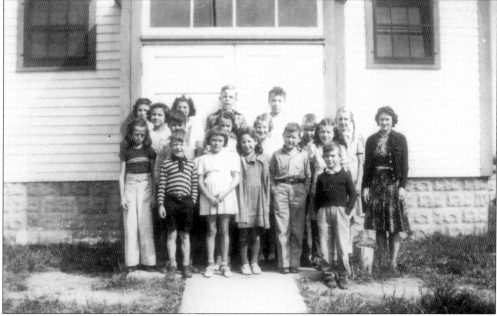

This photograph, taken in October of 1940, shows the remodeled front of the Sand Lake School. Picture here, from left to right, are: (front row) Marjorie Thompson, Tommy Alfredson, Magdeline ?, Marion Theehs, Lawrence (Buddy) Reidel, Albert Lucas, teacher Susanna Koehmotedt; (middle row) Audrey Kallal, Donald Kallal, Georgia Lee Reidel, Donna Pope, Howard Schwicht, Evelyn Schwicht; (back row) Charlotte Lucas, Jaqueline Kallal, unidentified, and unidentified.

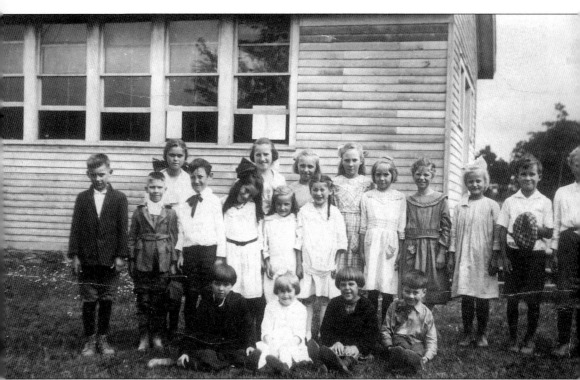

Monaville School District 40, one of the oldest in the township, was still thriving well into the 20th century. Similar to the one-room schoolhouses of the settler days, Monaville School operated until August 19, 1946, when it was also annexed by the Lake Villa School District. Unlike Sand Lake School, however, it was sold as a private residence in a matter of months. This picture was taken at the side of Monaville School. Though the date of the class is unknown, the teacher was Miss Louise Gerity. (Courtesy of Tom and Sharon Barnstable.)

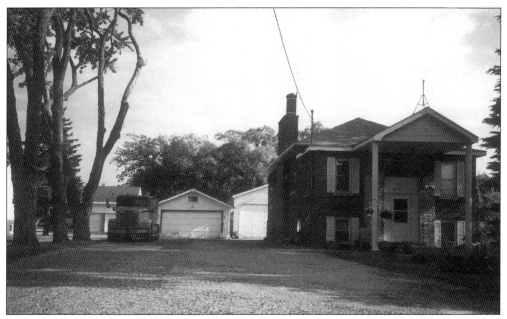

This photograph shows the old Cedar Lake Schoolhouse for District 32 on Petite Lake Road. This school was annexed by the Lake Villa School District in 1947, and remained in the district's possession until 1961, when it was also sold as a private residence. Many of Lake Villa's most prominent residents, such as Fred Nielsen, attended Cedar Lake School. (Photograph by author.)

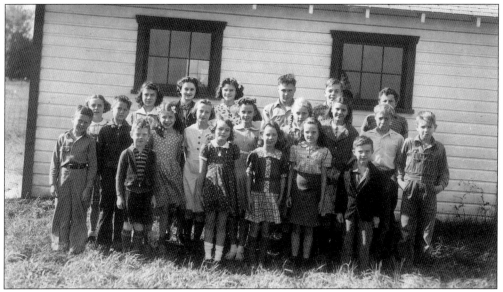

Many neighborhood schools within the township were annexed into Lake Villa School District during the 1940s. As the antiquated concept of the post office community faded into memory, keeping neighborhood schools operational was difficult. This push for annexation and consolidation ended in the creation of Lake Villa Consolidated School District 41 in 1954. Though these schools are only a memory, they recall a time when Lake Villa Township was identified by numerous trading communities and post office districts. This photograph shows one of the last classes of Sand Lake School.

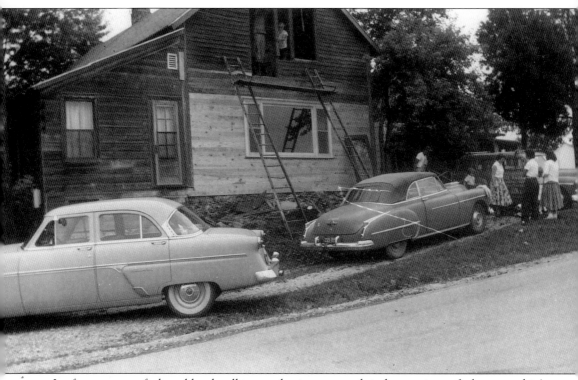

In fact, many of the old schoolhouses, businesses, and industry sites of the township's unincorporated areas still exist in the guise of private residences and abandoned structures. As the Village of Lake Villa crystallized as the economic center of the township, other area businesses closed quickly. Many of them, however, can be found all around the region if one knows where to look. This photograph from after World War II chronicles the renovation of the Tweed store, nexus of Monaville throughout the late 19th century. Presently, this home stands at the old heart of Monaville, an unassuming home along the quasi-rural Fairfield Road. (Courtesy of Tom and Sharon Barnstable.)

Especially in the unincorporated areas of the township, legends and stories have always played a prominent role in the construction of a collective past. Most (if not all) of these stories have some basis in truth. Stories of gangster hideouts, brothels, and piranhas dumped into Miltmore Lake, all become the common currency of many local residents. This is a photograph of the secluded island that separates Miltmore Lake from Fourth Lake. In the '60s, the home was allegedly owned by a segment of the ultra-libertarian John Birch Society. (Courtesy of Gwen Brysiewicz.)

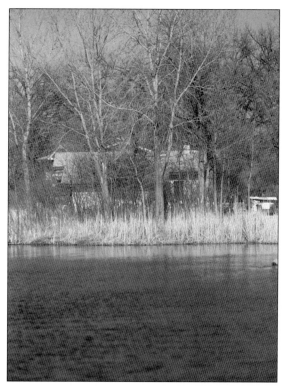

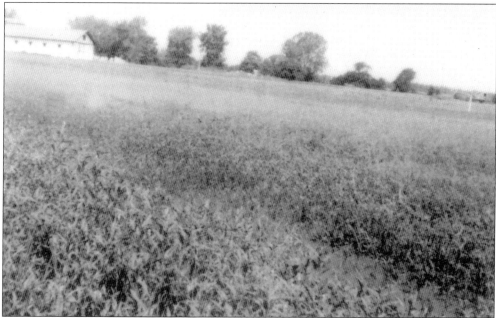

Not the entire unincorporated township was organized under small hamlets, however. Much of the eastern township was Ernst E. Lehmann's estate, a 240-acre dairy farm on Sand Lake called Lindenhurst. This estate would eventually produce not only the second incorporated village in the township, but also the township's most populous. Aptly named Lindenhurst, this photograph reveals the future site of the village.

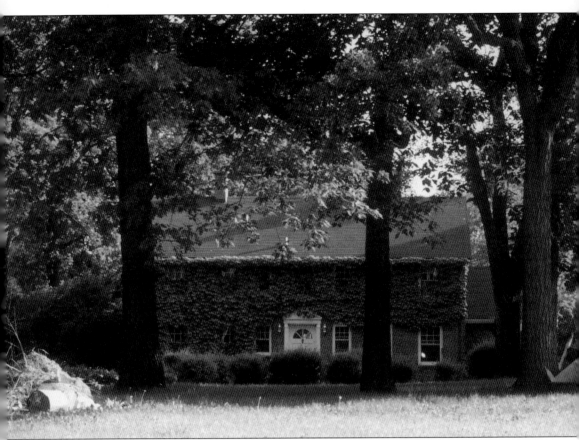

The Village of Lake Villa has always been quite distinguished from the surrounding region of the township. Throughout the first half of the 20th century, citizen's associations from West Miltmore, Venetian Village, and other neighborhood groups fought and worked diligently to bring good roads, working lights, clean and safe beaches, and a variety of other services to the region. As a result, the Village of Lake Villa and the rest of the township often found themselves at odds. One of the biggest supporters of the township's needs was Morton Engle, second-generation owner of the Nathan Hale Engle & Sons Real Estate Company. Not only was N.H. Engle & Sons responsible for creating West Miltmore, but it was also Morton Engle who led the 1952 subdivision of the Lindenhurst farm. And in the end, it would be Lindenhurst that changed the way Lake Villa dealt with the rest of the township. (Photograph by author.)

Six

CIVIC PRIDE

How would I describe Lake Villa? That it is a great little town, people like each other and are interested in the community. People help each other to succeed here, it's a great place to live.

—Amelia Saxe

Throughout the 20th century, one of the defining perceptions behind Lake Villa Township has been that of a close-knit community. Away from the bustle of the larger metropolitan area, those who lived and worked in the township knew most of the other people in the area. The economic and social dependency created by this relatively isolated region only intensified this sense of community.

The result has been a mixture of celebration and self-sacrifice. The infamous Lake Villa Days is one of metropolitan Chicago's longest running annual fairs, spanning most of the last century. Between the 1930s and the 1960s, many municipal services were completely performed by volunteer status workers dedicated to saving lives while making the community a better place to live. A strong VFW post was created and is maintained to this day, despite waning support for similar organizations all across the country.

Is there a particular name for this phenomenon? Possibly it is a feeling of civic pride, but that is only a speculation. Though Lake Villa Township is by no means the only American community to have a strong foundation of volunteerism, service, and celebration, the fervent combination of all three found in the township is something worth considering. If nothing else, the community spirit found throughout the township area serves as a reminder that though mansions and the resort complexes of the past may have disappeared, the community did not.

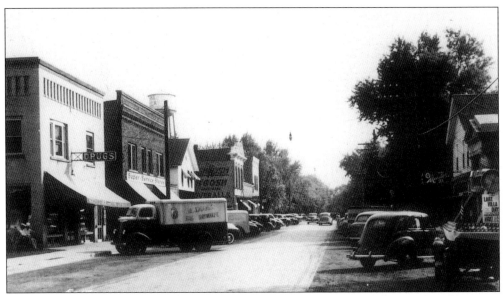

After years of muddy roads, downtown Lake Villa finally improved the roads of the area, making it more attractive to a new type of tourist, the day-tripper. This streetscape reveals an active downtown, despite the loss of past industry. (Note the Lake Villa Days advertisement on the far right.)

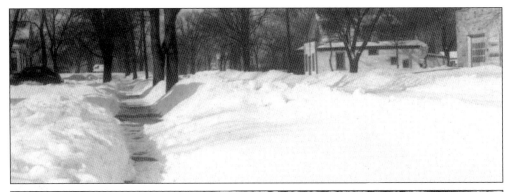

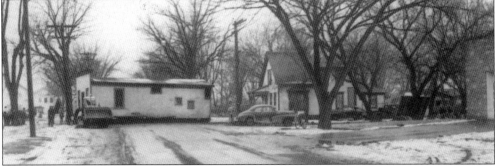

This photograph is actually a split print: the top photograph shows the Lake Villa Village Hall c.1943, just to the west of the fire department on Route 132, while the January 12, 1952, photograph below captures the building being moved. Not only did this small building house the Village Hall, but it also contained a fully functional jail.

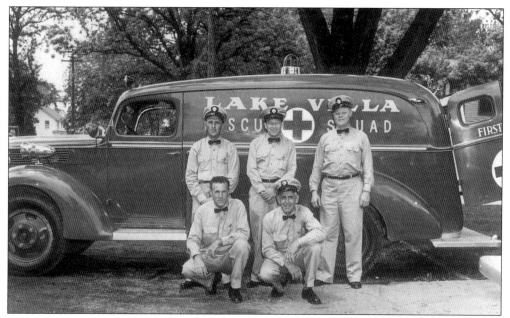

This photograph shows some of the charter members of the Lake Villa Rescue Squad, which was founded in the spring of 1956. From left to right are: (front row) Ben Cribb, Fred Popp Sr.; (back row) John Lynn, Jake Fish, and John Schueler. The only major pieces of equipment available to the beginning members of the rescue squad were a used vehicle from the Antioch Rescue Squad and an inhalator-resuscitator donated by the West Miltmore Community Association.

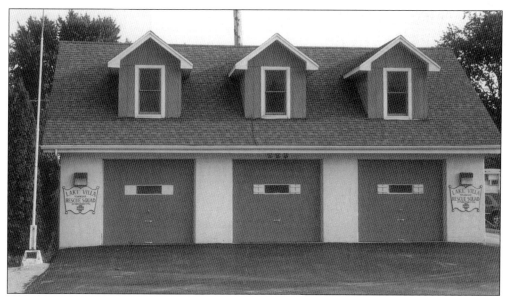

For many years, the volunteer-based Lake Villa Rescue Squad worked out of the Lake Villa Township Garage on Lake Avenue. By 1966, however, the squad had raised enough money to build the first Lake Villa Rescue Squad station pictured above. By the 1980s, the rescue squad, in concert with the fire department, constructed the current facility on Deep Lake Road and Route 132. The central location of this facility allows for more responsive service throughout the township. (Photograph by author.)

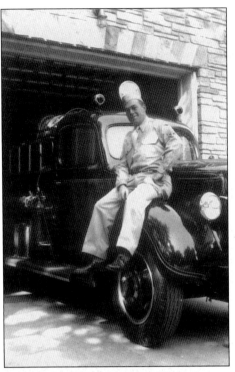

The Lake Villa Fire Department has also had a long history of volunteerism. Began in 1931, the original fire fighting equipment was housed in Morty Cannon's garage on Route 132 (Effinger's Hardware today). Pictured here is Frank Sciacero, one of the early members of the Lake Villa Fire Department. (Courtesy of Tom and Sharon Barnstable.)

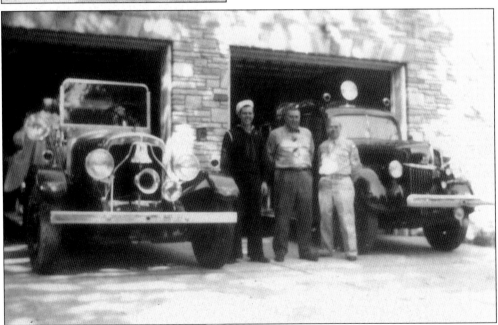

Soon after its inception, the Lake Villa Fire Department needed more space for its growing number of volunteers as well as the growing number of incidents occurring within the township. Between 1934 and 1940, the fire department worked out of the village hall. In 1940, the first segment of the current fire department station was completed. The station is pictured here with firefighters from left to right: unidentified, Ervin Barnstable, and Frank Sciacero. (Courtesy of Tom and Sharon Barnstable.)

One of the interesting facts about the fire department is how many multiple generations of local families have produced firefighters. Families such as the Naders, Slazes, Barnstables, Effingers, Hamlins, Schneiders, and Teltzs have all had more than one generation as a firefighter. Pride in the department is shown here as Dorothy Barnstable waves from a fire truck in a local parade c. 1964. (Courtesy of Tom and Sharon Barnstable.)

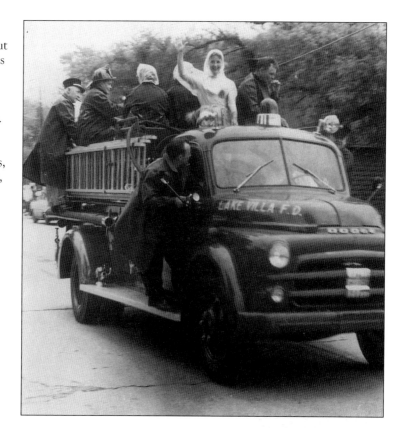

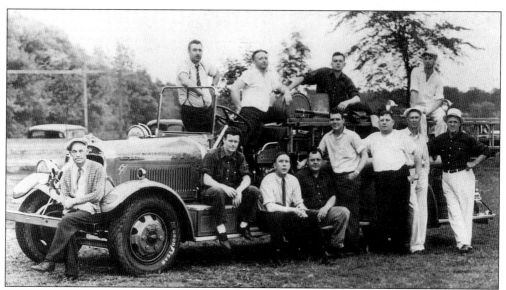

A common solution to the desire for strong municipal service is the creation of a volunteer force. Throughout the history of the Lake Villa Fire Department, many people have aided in the quest for a strong and safe community foundation. This is an early photograph of the Lake Villa Fire Department with their very first fire truck—a 1933 Pirsch, purchased for just over $5,000. (Courtesy of Bill and Carol Effinger.)

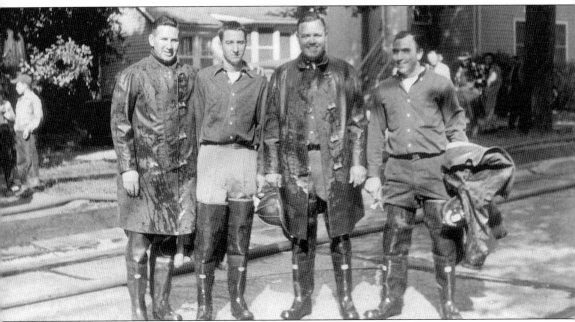

One tradition long celebrated by members of the Lake Villa Fire Department is the water hose fight. For many years, the last day of Lake Villa Days has been filled with teams squaring off against opponents in this particular tournament. Armed with only a firefighter's water hose, the goal is to push a barrel across the opponent's back line. On September 25, 1955, Lake Villa Fire Department members Clifford McCarthy, ? Petersen, (Elmer ?) Sheehan, and Ervin Barnstable Jr. became the water fight champions of Lake County. This photograph was taken at the Barrington, Illinois Invitational Water Fight Tournament. (Courtesy of Tom and Sharon Barnstable.)

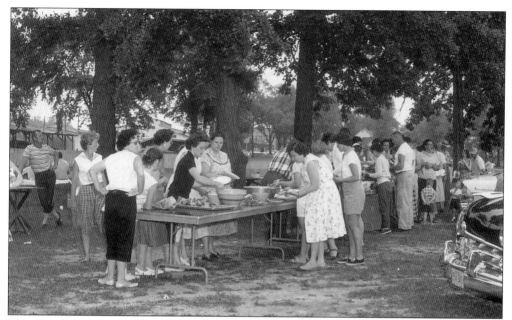

The Fireman's Picnic, a long tradition of the Lake Villa Fire Department, occurred for many years the day after the annual Lake Villa Days festivities. This photograph shows one such picnic from the late 1950s or early 1960s. (Courtesy of Tom and Sharon Barnstable.)

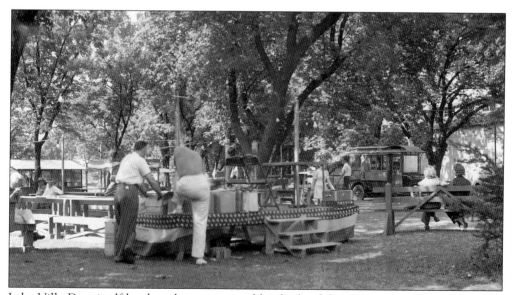

Lake Villa Days itself has long been sponsored by the local fire department. This photograph shows the setup of Lake Villa Days in Lehmann Park. Volunteers have been diligently setting and cleaning up for over 80 years. (Courtesy of Tom and Sharon Barnstable.)

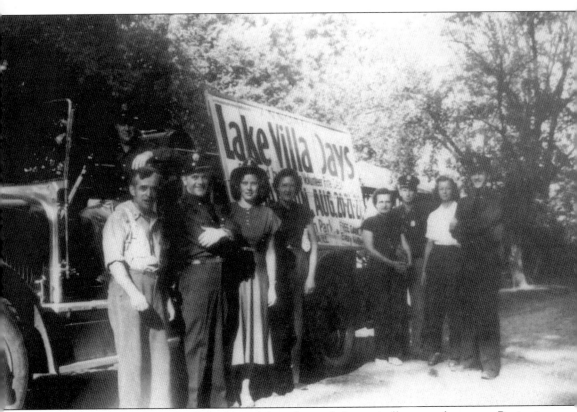

The Annual Lake Villa Days festival has changed dramatically over the years. Beginning around 1920, the original event was held for many years at the site of the current Lake Villa Post Office. The original fair consisted of horse shows, plow matches, and raffle prizes. As time has passed, Lake Villa Days has moved to Lehmann Park, added more carnival rides, games, and water fights. Horse shows and plow matches, on the other hand, are a thing of the past. This photograph depicts an advertisement for an early Lake Villa Days c. 1935. (Courtesy of Tom and Sharon Barnstable.)

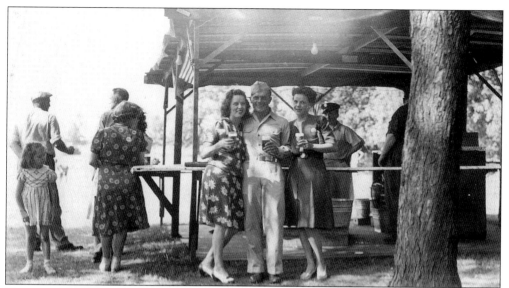

Not even World War II could stop Lake Villa Days. Throughout the war years, the festivities continued. When this photograph was taken in September of 1944, however, many of the enlisted men and women had returned home from war. (Courtesy of Tom and Sharon Barnstable.)

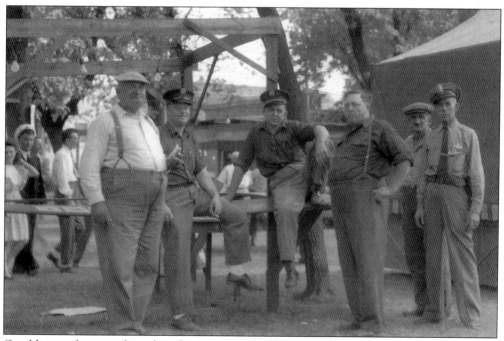

Gambling and gaming have long been a part of Lake Villa Days as well. In this photograph, a group of men sit beside the "Big Six" table, always a source of entertainment at the event. Pictured at the center of this group with his arm on his knee, Frank Slazes was one of the charter members of the Lake Villa Fire Department. (Courtesy of Tom and Sharon Barnstable.)

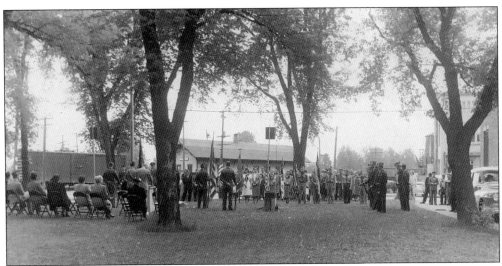

Another longtime tradition of the township is the annual Memorial Day Parade. After marching through downtown Lake Villa, a ceremony is held to honor those lost in war. This is a photograph of one such ceremony from the 1940s or 1950s. Even today, the Memorial Day ceremony is held at Lehmann Park. (Courtesy of Tom and Sharon Barnstable.)

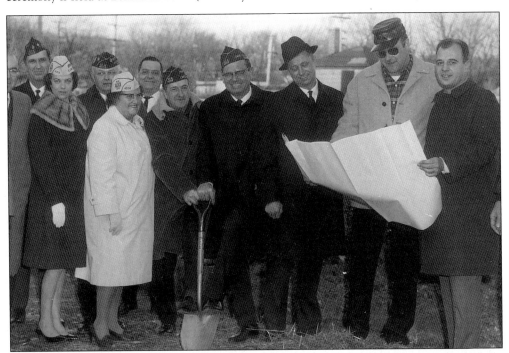

The Lake Villa Veterans of Foreign Wars Post 4308 was founded in November of 1954, to help consolidate the many veterans who traveled to VFW posts outside of the township. This photograph marks the 1956 "groundbreaking" of the VFW hall. In reality, the building for the hall already existed, but much renovation work was completed through dues, fund-raisers, and other events. Pictured here, from left to right, are: unidentified, Bob Whitmore, unidentified, unidentified, unidentified, Frances Sciacero, unidentified, Anthony Sciacero, Leo Kaisler, Donald Cremin, unidentified, and unidentified. (Courtesy of Tom and Sharon Barnstable.)

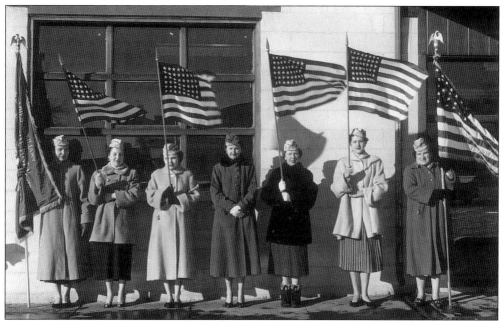

Men were not the only residents who took part in the activities of VFW Post 4308. A few years after the founding of the Lake Villa VFW, a Ladies Auxiliary post was created for the wives, sisters, and mothers of veterans. Pictured here, from left to right, are: Anna Nader, Arlyn Popp, Arlene Schneider, Rosella McCarthy (president), Cornelia Schneider, G. Peterson, and Frances Sciacero (first president). (Courtesy of Tom and Sharon Barnstable.)

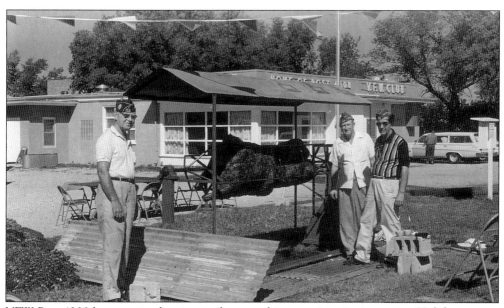

VFW Post 4308 has remained active in the township ever since its inception. Holiday parties, bingo, dances, sponsoring the Lake Villa Memorial Day Parade, and a host of charity work round out the extensive community outreach performed by the post. This photograph shows a pig roast from the summer of 1964. Pictured from left to right are Leo Kaisler, Anthony Sciacero, and unidentified. (Courtesy of Tom and Sharon Barnstable.)

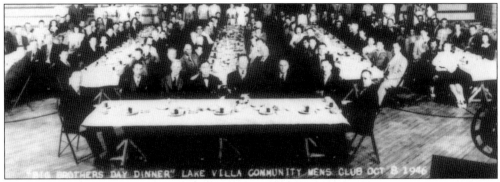

Community service and social organizations even financed major public structures. In 1949, the Lake Villa Community Men's Club (pictured here at a 1946 Big Brothers Day Dinner) offered to equip and maintain a public library. The group lived up to its word, and from 1949 to 1953, the Lake Villa Public Library worked out of the eastern room of the village hall. Operating on a complete volunteer basis, the Men's Club paid for books, heat, and janitorial services during this time.

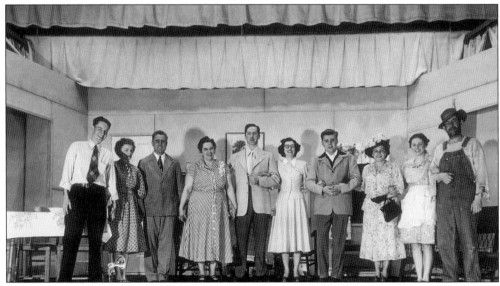

Community service, however, was not the only way residents took an active role in the community. Local adult actors, for instance, produced many theatrical productions during the 1940s and 1950s for the entertainment of the township. This photograph is a cast shot of a 1949 production, *The Cambells Are Coming*. (Courtesy of Bill and Carol Effinger.)

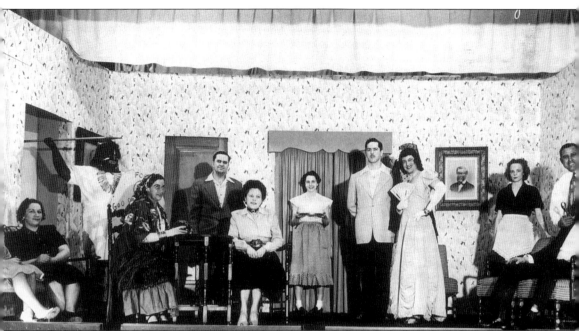

This photograph is another cast shot, but this is of the 1950 production of *Brides To Burn*. These theatrical productions were usually shown in Central School's (Pleviak) gymnasium, which was built in 1939. Primarily light-hearted comedies and musicals, these productions were known to draw large crowds. The spaciousness of the gym made it ideal for many local community events. Aside from the shows and musicals, many residents recall dances for teenagers and adults as well as large bingo and poker tournaments. For a while, Central School served as the de facto Lake Villa community center. (Courtesy of Bill and Carol Effinger.)

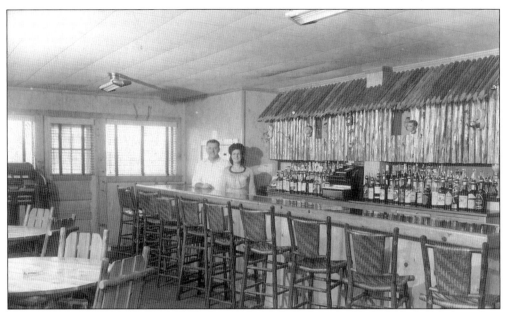

Even the local tavern scene was full of interesting destinations, whether for the local resident or the weekend tourist. Sherry's, a tavern and liquor store that opened right after World War II, offered food, ice cream, and spirits in a festive atmosphere. This photograph shows the proprietors, Ed and Evelyn Sherry, behind their bar. (Courtesy of Tom and Sharon Barnstable.)

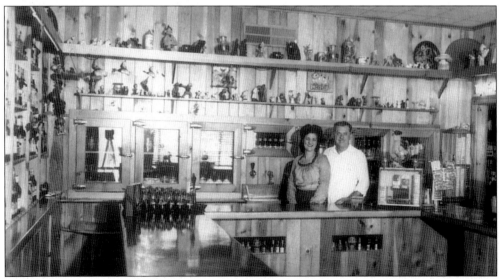

Aside from Sherry's (pictured here in a 1948 Christmas card), many resorts and taverns throughout the township continued to draw crowds. Many were located on the lakes, giving patrons access to the same amenities afforded Lake Villa Hotel guests a half century before. For some establishments, the weekend Chicago crowd was crucial for good business. (Courtesy of Tom and Sharon Barnstable.)

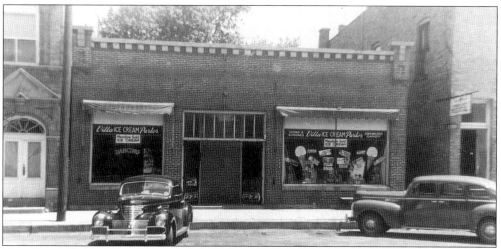

Not all establishments were geared toward an adult crowd, however. The Villa Ice Cream Parlor became the hangout for many young residents during this time. Not only did the parlor serve ice cream and fountain sodas, but it also had dancing for any who were interested. (Courtesy of Bill and Carol Effinger.)

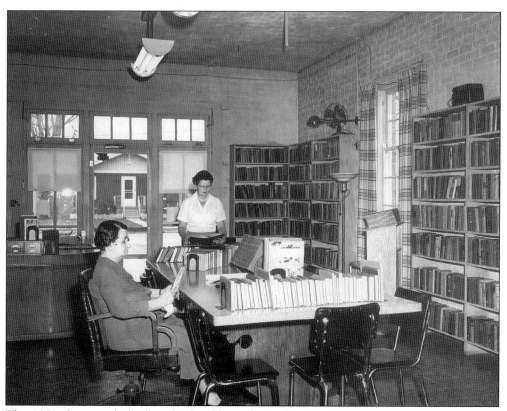

This 1952 photograph displays the first library, housed in the Lake Villa Village Hall. Mrs. Lois Kerr (standing) was the first Lake Villa librarian, a volunteer position at the time. The patron in this photo is Mrs. Kerr's mother, Mrs. Milligan. Within the span of a few years, the resources and demand for a public library would force the library to expand—down the street.

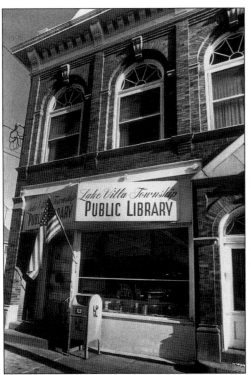

In 1957, the Lake Villa Township Public Library moved to its 117 Cedar Avenue location, pictured here. Ever since, however, a booming township population as well as the desire for new amenities has kept the library on the move. In 1980, the library moved to a much larger facility at the intersection of Deep Lake Road and Route 132. In the late 1990s, this facility was significantly renovated to keep up with the demands of the township. (Courtesy of the *News-Sun*.)

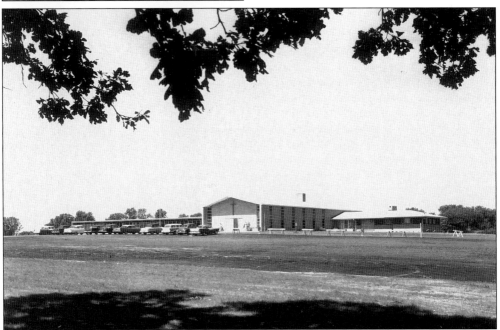

On June 29, 1955, territory for the Prince of Peace Catholic Church was carved out of St. Peter Church territory in Antioch and St. Gilbert Church territory in Grayslake. The pictured church opened in the fall of 1957, as did the attached elementary school. Located on the southeastern corner of Route 83 and Route 132, this photograph was taken before the construction of a new church addition in 1980.

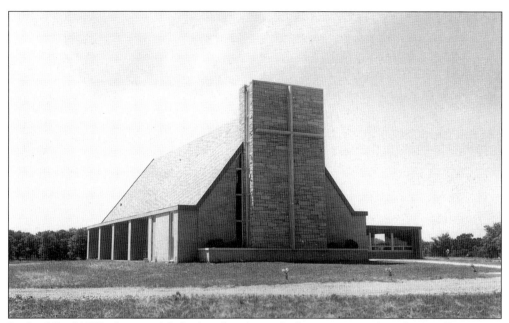

In the fall of 1958, this new Methodist church was built to accommodate the rapidly growing congregation of the "church on the hill." In 1968, a parsonage was built, and in 1987, this new church was remodeled and updated. Pictured here on McKinley Avenue, the new Methodist church now handles all services of the congregation. The "church on the hill," now over 125 years old, is currently a private residence.

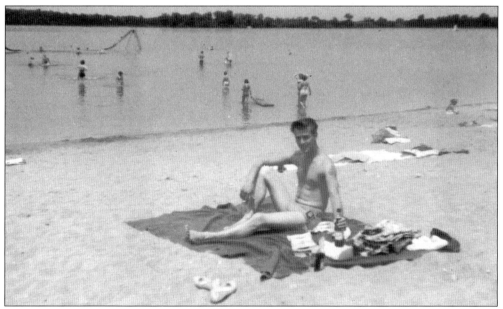

Long after the heyday of rail-based resorting, the township continued to enjoy an influx of urban visitors looking to escape to the countryside in their automobiles. Some recall traffic on Route 83 backed up for miles if it was a beautiful summer weekend. The Sherwood family ran two major parks up until the 1970s–80s. Pictured here is local resident Richard Tranberg spending a day on the beach. (Courtesy of Gwen Brysiewicz.)

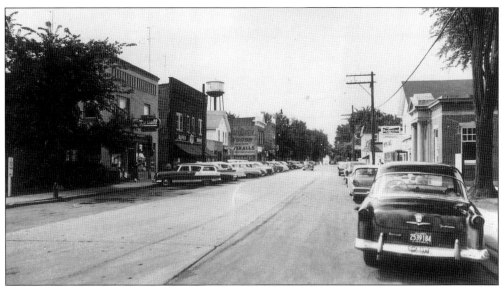

Regardless of its waning prominence in the regional industry of metropolitan Chicago, Lake Villa Township held together throughout the 20th century by relying on neighbors and creating a close-knit community. Though some are critical of what they considered to be control by a few privileged local leaders, it is undeniable that the community leaders used their power and influence to create many positive and lasting improvements on the township. (Courtesy of Bill and Carol Effinger.)

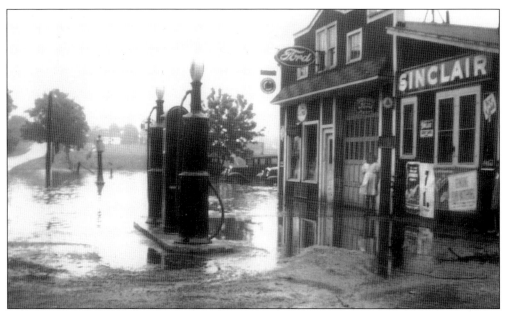

Though civic pride in all its forms was prevalent throughout the township and village of Lake Villa, other forces were conspiring against the local business leaders of the community. Lindenhurst, the 1952 subdivision at the township's eastern end, rapidly became a second population concentration in the region. Furthermore, its new shopping plaza was more than many businesses could compete with, transforming Lake Villa's bustling downtown into a quiet street. (Courtesy of Tom and Sharon Barnstable.)

Seven

LINDENHURST

For years, people would do all of their shopping at Daalgard's (in Lake Villa). When the Linden Plaza came in though, people would only stop by Daalgard's for the specials.

—Marilyn Brysiewicz

Out of nowhere. This phrase has often been used to describe the way in which Lindenhurst stormed onto the maps of Lake Villa Township. In 1951, Lindenhurst was the agrarian remains of Ernst E. Lehmann's farm by the same name. By 1956, local citizens were voting for incorporation to create tighter controls on the explosive growth within the nascent community.

The short journey from farm to village began abruptly in 1952, when N.H. Engle & Sons began subdividing the former Lehmann estate. During this time, the greater Chicago metropolitan area was experiencing a huge postwar housing boom as former urbanites chose to make permanent homes in suburbia and its outskirts. The idyllic family homes of Lindenhurst offered the perfect solution for a home-hungry nation.

Despite the impact of these new neighborhoods in Lake Villa Township, the most significant change created by Lindenhurst may have been the Linden Plaza. Opened in 1960, this shopping center was the first of its kind within the township. Its arrival changed the precarious balance of available services and goods that had been established within the township for decades. Local businesses, either unable to compete with prices or the novelty of the plaza, closed in record number. In addition, the exponential growth of Lindenhurst quickly eclipsed the population of the Village of Lake Villa. After 70 years of domination in township affairs, a new village rivaled that claim. Subsequent years have found people at all levels of the two communities working together to maintain a shared sense of the township area, while others identify themselves exclusively with an incorporated village, be it Lake Villa or Lindenhurst.

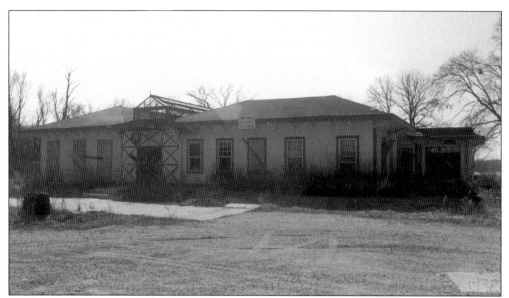

Ernst E. Lehmann's Lindenhurst Farm was not only a working dairy farm. The main house (pictured above) was a white stucco ranch, with a large atrium in the center of the home. In addition to the dairy production, Ernst E. pampered and raised Pekinese show dogs. After Lehmann passed away in 1930, his estate passed from owner to owner. It was both a restaurant and a nursing home in subsequent years, but today it is known as R.J.'s Eatery on the corner of Granada and Route 132. (Courtesy of Lindenhurst Village Hall.)

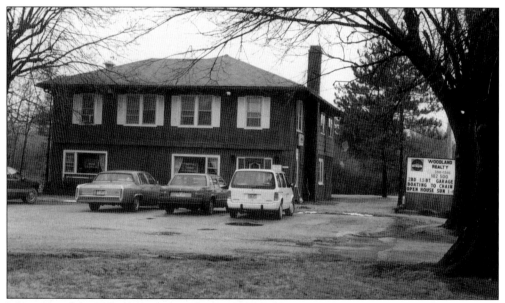

Like most of the Lehmann estates, the Lindenhurst Farm consisted of many buildings. Across Route 132 from the main house once stood tenant houses, a main barn, a small bull barn, a creamery, an icehouse (now the rear part of the Lindenhurst Men's Club), a milk house, and a wagon barn. Some of these secondary structures exist into the present, such as the Woodland Realty office on Route 132, just west of the intersection of Granada and Route 132. (Courtesy of Lindenhurst Village Hall.)

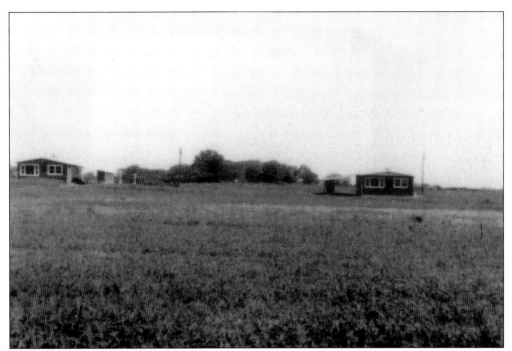

When Morton Engle subdivided the former Lindenhurst Farm, he immediately transformed the eastern end of Lake Villa Township from an agrarian region to a residential one. This photograph shows the early stages of subdivision. The houses pictured are on Burr Oak Lane. (Courtesy of Lindenhurst Village Hall.)

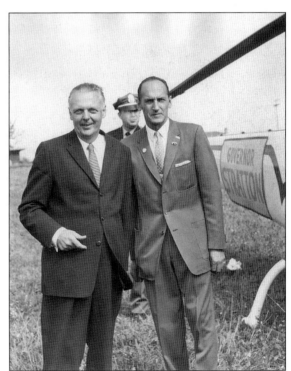

When the Linden Plaza shopping center was being constructed, Illinois governor Bill Stratton dropped in by helicopter to see the area. The governor had familial ties to Lake Villa Township; his grandfather John Stratton led the petition to form the township, and he was also its first supervisor in 1913. (Courtesy of Lindenhurst Village Hall.)

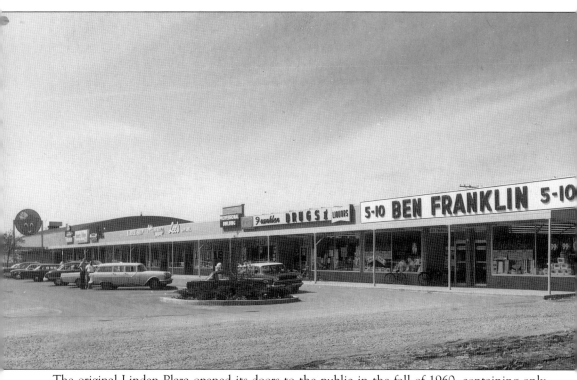

The original Linden Plaza opened its doors to the public in the fall of 1960, containing only four stores: a Piggly Wiggly grocery store, Slove's Bakery, Village Laundry, and Linden Cleaners. Within a couple of years, however, the plaza expanded again, this time adding a barbershop, a clothing store, and a large Ben Franklin pharmacy (pictured above). The arrival of this commercial business center not only solidified Lindenhurst's place within Lake Villa Township, but it also put added strain on the small businesses that lined Cedar Avenue in Lake Villa. Furthermore, the demographics of the township were also changing with the growth of Lindenhurst. In general, younger families began moving in to Lindenhurst, affecting everything from the school PTO board to the kinds of businesses brought to the area.

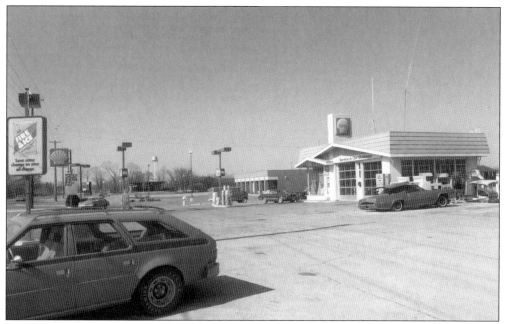

Thor's Shell on the northeastern corner of Lindenhurst Drive and Route 132 was the first business established in Lindenhurst, opening in the fall of 1958. Changing hands more than once, it was torn down in the 1980s to make room for a renovated and expanded Eagle grocery store. (Courtesy of Lindenhurst Village Hall.)

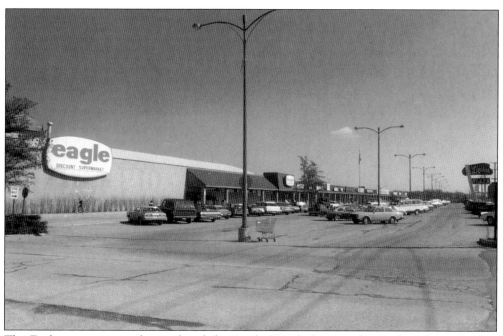

The Eagle grocery store that replaced the Piggly Wiggly became the Linden Plaza's flagship store for many years. Shown here before its 1980s expansion, Eagle moved in the late 1990s to a new location further west on the corner of Route 132 and Munn Road. Currently, the space which formerly housed the grocer is empty and for sale. (Courtesy of Lindenhurst Village Hall.)

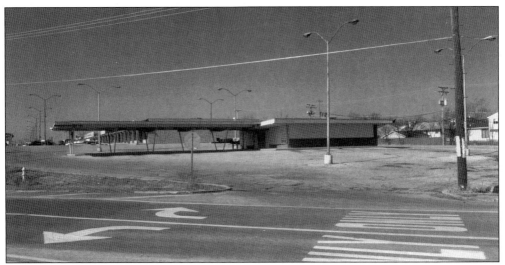

As the 1960s wore on, Linden Plaza continued to grow, ending at a Dog & Suds Drive-in on the corner of Route 132 and Sand Lake Road. Novel restaurants and businesses filled the plaza, attracting many residents to shop locally. In this picture, the Dog & Suds is closed, but the building remains. Today, the building has since been razed, and the plaza and a convenience store utilize this space. (Courtesy of Lindenhurst Village Hall.)

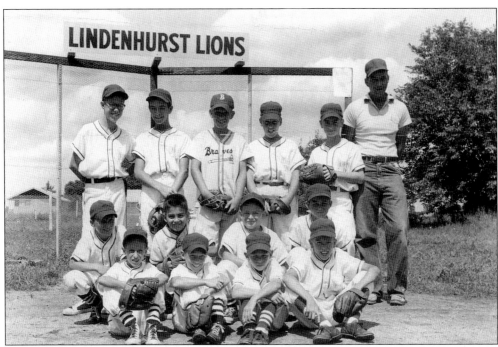

In addition to residential and commercial growth, Lindenhurst quickly developed a strong civic community as well. The Lindenhurst Lions were the first little league team for the community. Pictured from left to right are: (front row) unidentified, Mickey Caldwell, Bob Brendel, unidentified; (middle row) unidentified, unidentified, unidentified, Fabry, ? Singer; (back row) Joe Downs, Gene Lucas, Toby Henry, Bill Brendel, Bob Randall, and coach Ray Caldwell. (Courtesy of Lindenhurst Village Hall.)

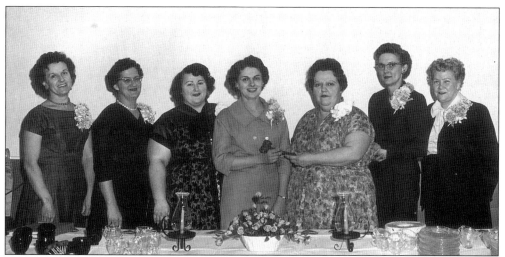

Lindenhurst also developed as a strong political and social center, which included women. This is a photograph of Lois Flanagan being installed as the new president of the Lindenhurst Women's Club, accepting the gavel from Grace Slove, the previous president. Pictured from left to right are: Mary Zanck, unidentified, Lou Stanley, Lois Flanagan, Grace Slove, Betty Ireland, and Dorothy Verdick. (Courtesy of Lindenhurst Village Hall.)

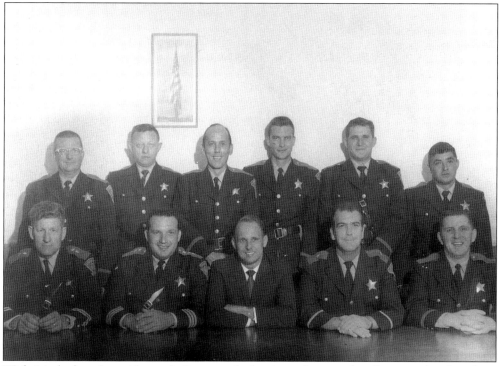

With Lindenhurst's rapid population growth, having a large and well-prepared police force became a priority for the village. This photograph shows the Lindenhurst Police Department in full uniform. Longtime Lindenhurst police chief Ronald Coles is pictured here, second from the left in the front row. (Courtesy of Lindenhurst Village Hall.)

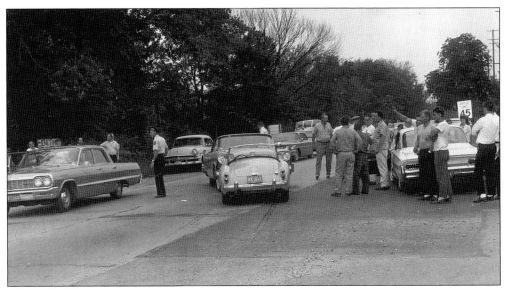

Another effect of Lindenhurst's rapid population growth was increased traffic on the township roadways within a matter of a few years. With this rapid change came an increase in automobile accidents, like the one pictured here. This accident occurred in July of 1964, on Route 132 near the Linden Plaza. (Courtesy of Lindenhurst Village Hall.)

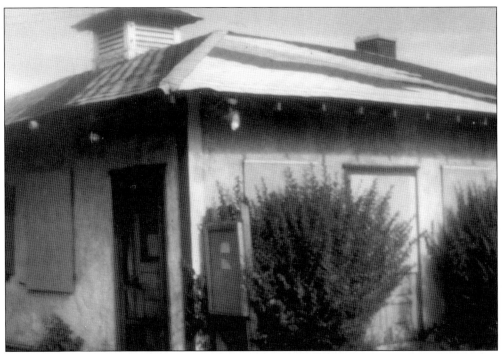

The original Lindenhurst Village Hall was a primitive structure. In the early 1970s, it was decided that a new, grand village hall was necessary to keep up with the growing community. For a time, the village hall was located in Linden Plaza while construction on the new village hall progressed. This photograph shows the original Lindenhurst Village Hall before its demolition. (Courtesy of Lindenhurst Village Hall.)

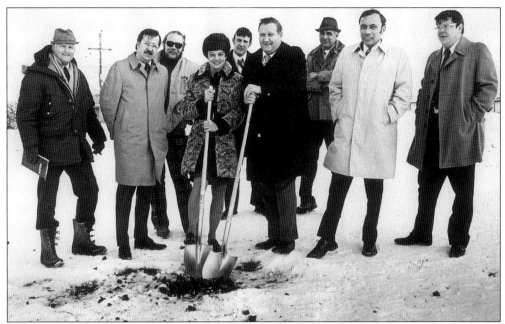

Groundbreaking for the new Lindenhurst Village Hall in March of 1974 was met with much fanfare. Those who attended the ceremonies are, from left to right: (holding shovels) Judy Kempher, village clerk; and Ted Flanagan, mayor; (back row) building inspector Douglass Getchell, trustee Al Ott, trustee Fred Fabry, Dennis Powell from the Lake Villa Bank, contractor Don Henderson, trustee Robert Ratch, and trustee James Johnson. (Courtesy of Lindenhurst Village Hall.)

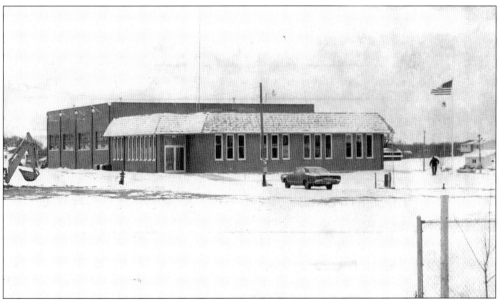

When the new village hall was finally completed in early 1975, it not only housed village official offices. The complex also included council rooms, the Lindenhurst Police Department, as well as a maintenance garage. Since then, additional facilities have been constructed around the Lindenhurst Village Hall. (Courtesy of Lindenhurst Village Hall.)

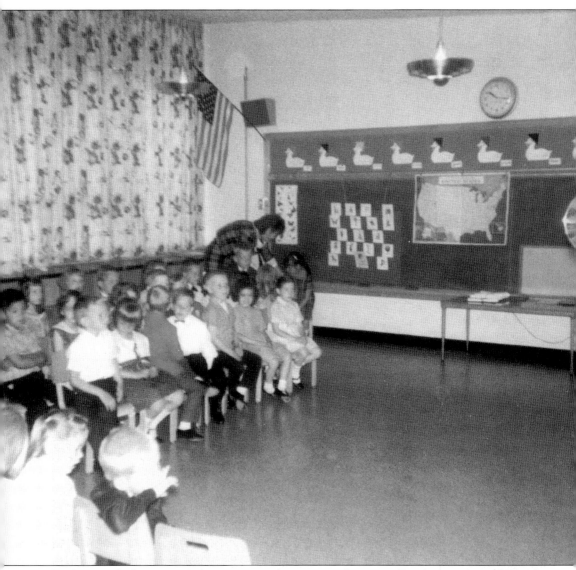

Expansion of other municipal services was also necessary because of Lindenhurst's rapid growth. For instance, B.J. Hooper School was constructed from a parcel of Howard Bonner's farmland on the corner of Beck and Sand Lake Roads. The school opened its doors in September of 1958, and received its first addition by 1961. Though Lake Villa School District had been in the process of annexing and consolidating the various neighborhood schools, it was clear that Lindenhurst needed a school built within its village limits. This picture shows a classroom in B.J. Hooper School from the mid-1960s. (Courtesy of Gwen Brysiewicz)

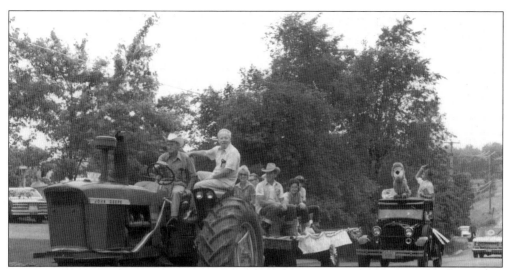

In later years, Lindenhurst has even created its own community celebrations distinct from the traditions of the earlier village. In this 1980s parade down Beck Road, homage is paid to the area's agrarian past by one of the few remaining local farmers. It is usually more profitable for a farmer to sell to developers than it is to continue working the land. (Courtesy of Lindenhurst Village Hall.)

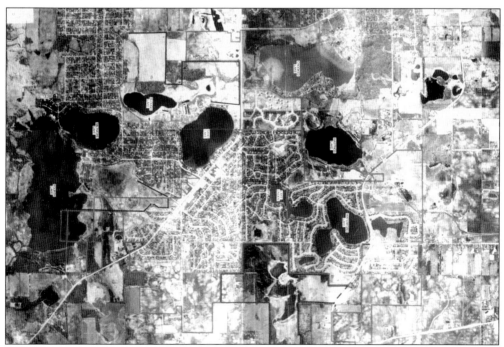

Fueled by the suburbanization of America, Lindenhurst's many wooded streets and quiet lakes have made rapidly settling of the area an easy task. Not as easy are the municipal headaches that come with an exploding population: road safety, commute times, pollution, smart development, and blight have all contributed to resident and official dissatisfaction from time to time. This aerial shot of Lindenhurst (outlined above) reveals both the many lakes and the many roads of the upstart area. (Courtesy of Lindenhurst Village Hall.)

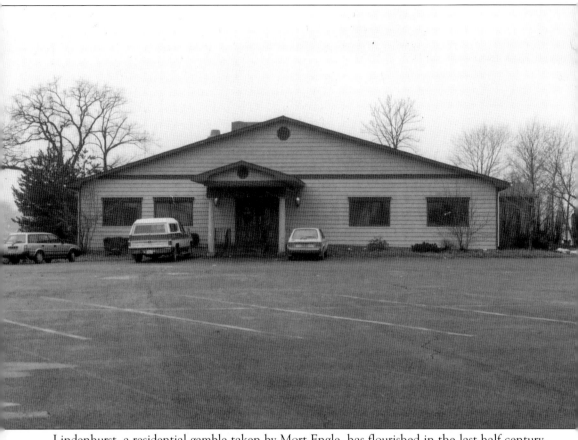

Lindenhurst, a residential gamble taken by Mort Engle, has flourished in the last half century. Not only did it create a brand new village from an aging farm, but also it has raised the general level of Lake Villa Township's prestige. Though the Village of Lake Villa's median price for housing stock hovered around $131,000 in 1990, many of the average homes in Lindenhurst were averaging twice as much. This could have been seen as help or a hindrance to the community of Lake Villa, but in the last decade of the 20th century, Lake Villa has had a population explosion and housing stock revolution in its own right. Currently, all of Lake Villa Township is being transformed as the metropolitan fringe of Chicago makes its way towards the region. In the coming years, Lake Villa, Lindenhurst, and the unincorporated hamlets will all have to redefine themselves once again. (Courtesy of Lindenhurst Village Hall.)

Eight
REJUVENATION

While I think it's good the town is growing so rapidly, I don't really like some of the neighborhoods that are going up because the developers are not putting enough time, thought, or creativity into what's being built.

—Aja Brown

I think all of the development around here is great. I can't quite get over the way it's building up, you know. Very good for the whole community.

—Dorothy Langbein

In the last 25 years, the history of Lake Villa Township has been one of rapid growth and acceptance of a new, suburban identity. During the 1980s, Lake Villa's population grew by 95 percent. Between the years of 1975 and 2000, the village grew by 164 percent. Lake Villa Township, on the other hand, grew by a staggering 359 percent during this same period.

What has caused this substantial and rapid growth in the region? There are a few factors that have converged to create this phenomenon. First, the constant spread of the Chicago metropolitan area has begun to reach Lake Villa Township. The region is on the metropolitan fringe, so to speak. Head away from the city and one quickly reaches rural, independent towns; head towards the city and one enters a contiguous sea of crowded municipalities. Second, the rise of Gurnee as an edge city (a large municipality on the "edge" of a long established metropolitan area that contains a substantial amount of white-collar businesses, corporate parks, and shopping malls) has meant major growth for the surrounding region, including Lake Villa Township.

Some of the effects of this growth have been drastic, such as the rapid development of businesses all along the Route 83 corridor through Lake Villa. Other effects have been almost reactionary. For instance, in 1986, Lake Villa Township's various hamlets attempted to become a third incorporated entity called Liberty Lakes. The point of such a move was to protect the rural nature of the hamlets in the wake of massive annexation and development by both Lindenhurst and Lake Villa. In the end, the case (Lindenhurst and Lake Villa fought Liberty Lakes) made it all the way the Illinois Supreme Court. The court disallowed the hamlets to pursue the idea, but for a time it seemed a legitimate possibility.

Overall, this unheralded surge of economic, residential, and municipal development is neither good nor bad for the community. Rather, how the township deals with the pressures of this development is all that matters. Rejuvenation of business and of residential development is certainly pervasive throughout Lake Villa Township. What remains to be seen, however, is whether this translates into a rejuvenation of community as well.

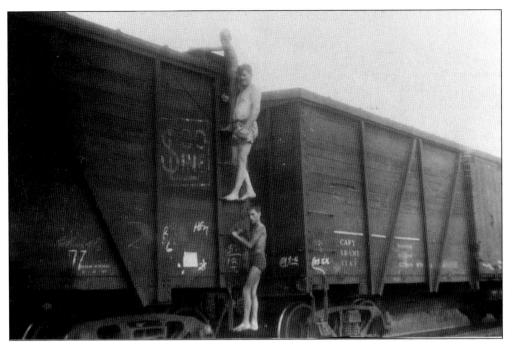

As the 1950s turned into the 1960s, the significance of the Lake Villa passenger train, a gradually declining industry for 40 years, precipitously dropped away. When the last passenger train came through Lake Villa on September 24, 1964, an era had passed. The railroad, once the reason for Lake Villa's existence, was no longer necessary or useful to the township. Pictured here are some people posing on a stopped Soo Line train through Lake Villa. (Courtesy of Gwen Brysiewicz.)

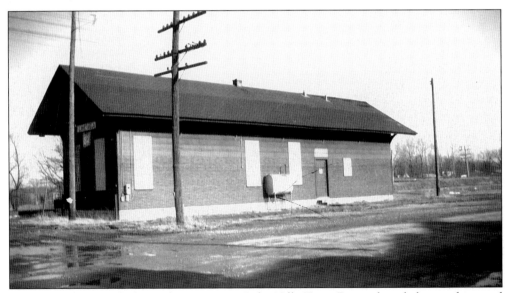

This 1964 photograph shows the once great Lake Villa Train Depot, boarded up and ignored by the community. The original caption on the back of this photograph states: "This was the busiest place in Lake Villa for years—no trains stop here anymore—It just doesn't seem possible. . . ."

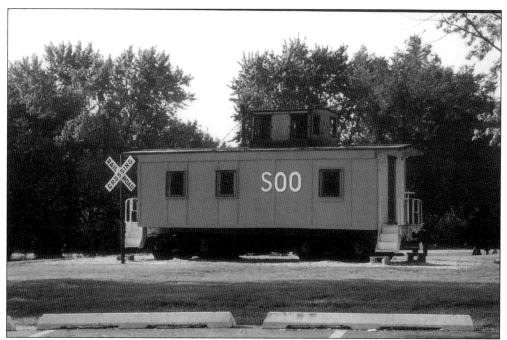

As a reminder of the past importance of the train, the Village of Lake Villa in the 1970s attempted to secure, with the help of the train company, a Soo Line caboose. The plan to put the caboose in Lehmann Park never came to fruition, but Ronald Coles as the Lake Villa Township Supervisor was able to get the caboose for the Lake Villa Township Park. Located at the intersection of Fairfield and Route 132, the caboose can still be seen today. (Photograph by author.)

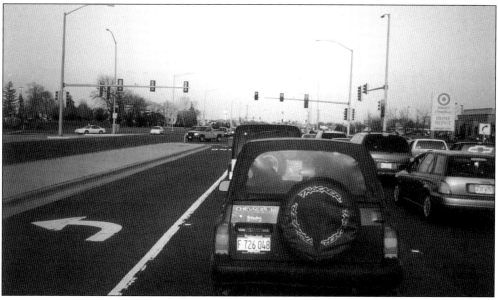

The explosion of Gurnee (particularly around the area of Gurnee Mills shopping center pictured here) in the last decade has contributed greatly to the population surge currently being experienced by Lake Villa Township. Most residents do their primary shopping at either Gurnee Mills or the Round Lake Beach business district along Rollins Road. (Photograph by author.)

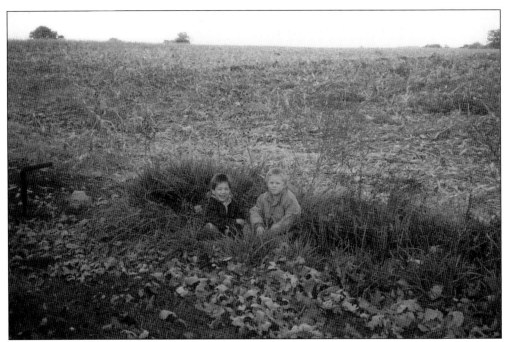

The transformation from an agrarian township to a suburban township has been a rapid process. Howard Bonner's Farm in Lindenhurst is in the background of this photograph. As late as the early 1990s, Bonner's farm was fully functional. Pictured here from left to right are Neil Brysiewicz and Timothy Bridges. (Courtesy of Walter and Gwen Brysiewicz.)

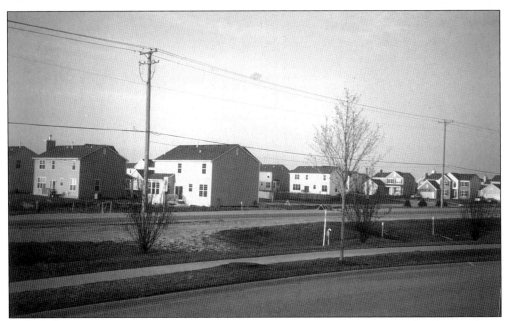

Today, Bonner's Farm has been converted into the housing development pictured here. This is just one example of many area farms that have been transformed into subdivisions within the last decade. The rows of large homes and townhomes pictured here have created a radically new aesthetic for the Lindenhurst area in a short amount of time. (Photograph by author.)

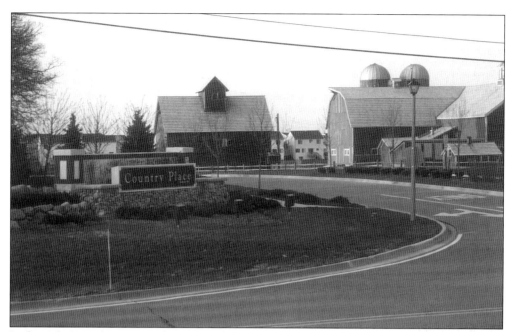

In fact, the transformation of Bonner's farmstead into subdivisions has been a unique case in preservation. Though now called Country Place, the buildings of Bonner's farm have been preserved at the entrance to the community. This mix of rural and suburban in many ways symbolizes the mixed desires of the township at large. (Photograph by author.)

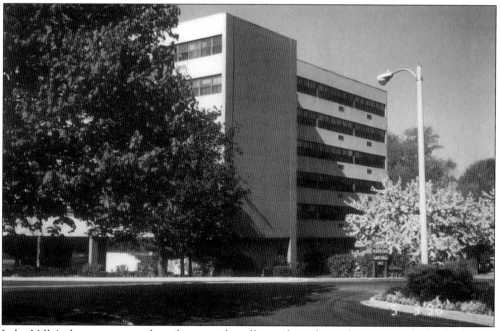

Lake Villa's downtown area has also seen the effects of rapid population growth. In the last 20 years, many services and products have become available in the area again. Pictured here is Cedar Village, a retirement community on Route 83. In fact, Cedar Village stands exactly on the site of the old Lake Villa Hotel.

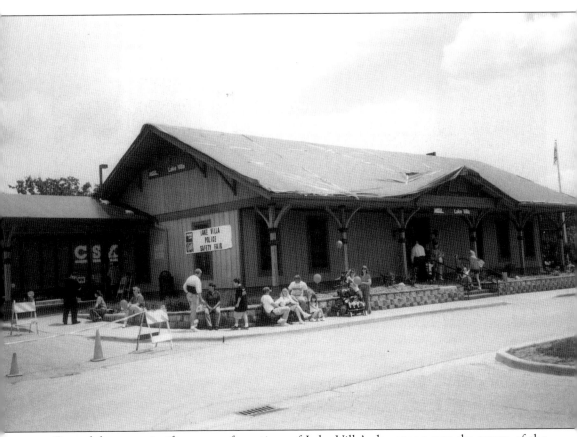

One of the most significant transformations of Lake Villa's downtown was the return of the passenger train. In 1996, Metra commuter rail started the North Central Line on the tracks of the Wisconsin Central. Of all the communities on the rail, Lake Villa was finished first with its brand new station, built as a replica of the original grand Lake Villa Depot. Though the train has been a big success in the community since its return, most traffic now heads towards the city, not away from it. The Lake Villa Police Safety Fair, along with many other community events, are often held at the new train depot. (Photograph by author.)

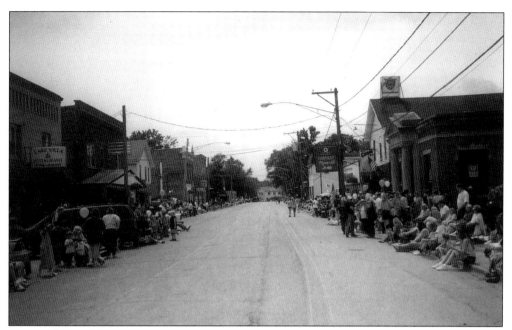

Even with all of the rapid changes taking place in the township, Lake Villa's main street, Cedar Avenue, has remained remarkably similar for over 100 years. Pictured here is a crowd gathered for the 2001 Memorial Day Parade, a special parade because Lake Villa celebrated its Centennial in 2001. (Photograph by author.)

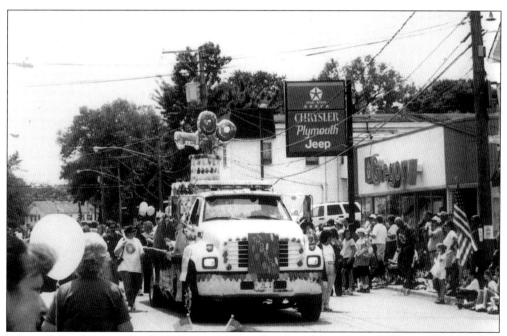

Many of the floats at the 2001 Memorial Day Parade celebrated the Village of Lake Villa's Centennial with floats such as the birthday cake and balloon pictured here. In addition to the parade, the Lake Villa Village Hall planned many events to celebrate the centennial throughout the year. (Photograph by author.)

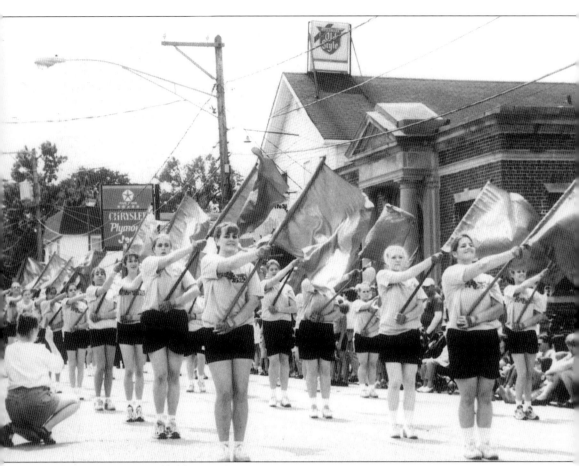

The Antioch School District Color Guard team was one of the highlights at the Lake Villa Memorial Day Parade. Lake Villa Township students attend high school in Grayslake, Antioch, or Grant High School Districts. As a result, the surrounding communities must work in close concert with one another. Nevertheless, many people desire a Lake Villa-Lindenhurst High School for the township. With the construction of a second Antioch High School under way, however, this prospect seems unlikely in the near future. The brick building in this photograph was the original Lake Villa Bank. Now vacant, some are interested in transforming the structure into a local historical society. (Photograph by author.)

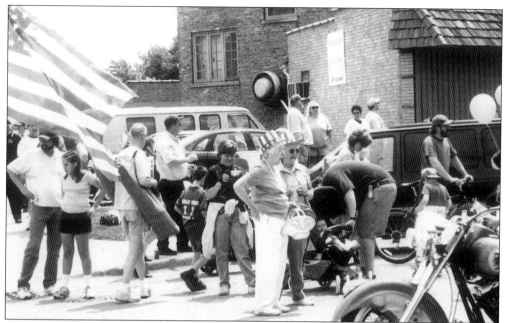

Watching the Memorial Day festivities, many of the eldest generation have stories, anecdotes, and information for the curious ear. At the center of this picture is Dorothy Langbein (holding a basket), daughter of the prominent Lake Villa leader Bert J. Hooper. As the parade passes by, Mrs. Langbein stands in front of the building that once housed her father's pharmacy. Today it is the Lake Villa Restaurant. (Photograph by author.)

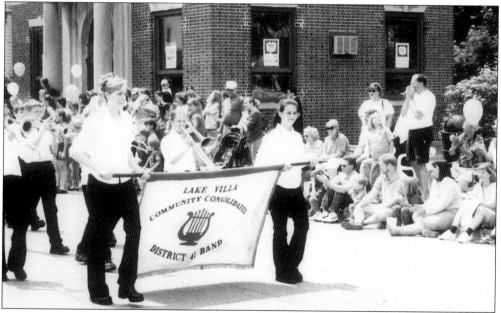

The Lake Villa District 41 Band plays in the Memorial Day Parade every year. In recent years, the rapid population growth has forced the school district to construct major additions on older township schools (Joseph J. Pleviak School, B.J. Hooper School, Palombi Middle School) as well as create a fourth area school, the William L. Thompson School. (Photograph by author.)

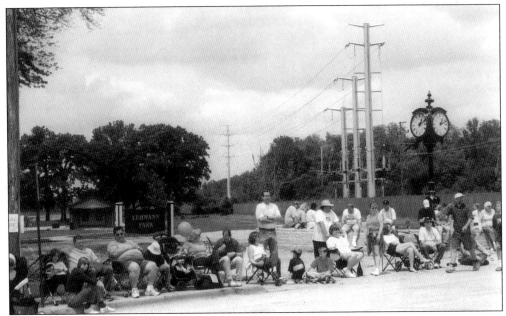

In addition to the many celebratory events for Lake Villa's Centennial year, other projects have been undertaken around the community to rejuvenate the original downtown and other older areas of the community. Lehmann Park, a mainstay of the downtown for many years, has been expanded. To the right is the Centennial clock, a testament to a century of changes undergone by the community. (Photograph by author.)

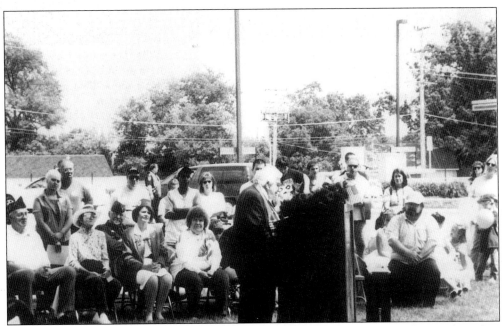

As is tradition, the 2001 Memorial Day Parade ended with a ceremony to honor those lost through the ravages of war. Held at Lehmann Park, the ceremony featured State Senator Adeline Geo-Karis. In her speech, she especially remembers those who fought in World War II and her own memories of the event. (Photograph by author.)

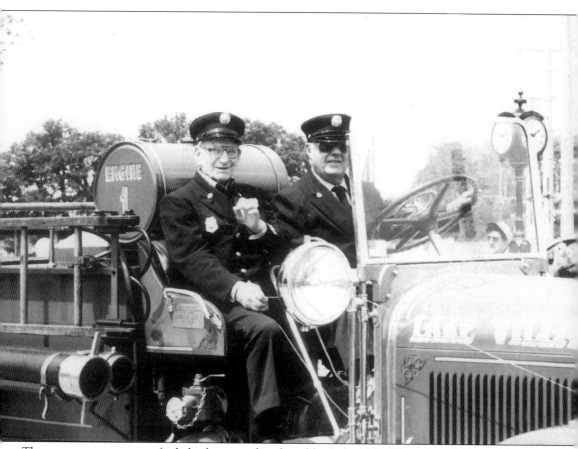

There are many ways to find the history of a place like Lake Villa Township. Old records, buildings, images—these are all ways to get closer to the past lives and places that have inexorably shaped the present. It is people, however, that provide the most vibrant link to the past. Perhaps then the most poignant reminder of Lake Villa's Centennial is oldest living resident and original member of the fire department, Joe Nader. At 95 years old, Mr. Nader rides atop the fire department's first purchase, a still pristine 1933 Pirsch fire truck. Quite possibly more than anyone else, Mr. Nader has seen, felt, and experienced the many changes that have marked the last century of Lake Villa Township. (Photograph by author.)

127

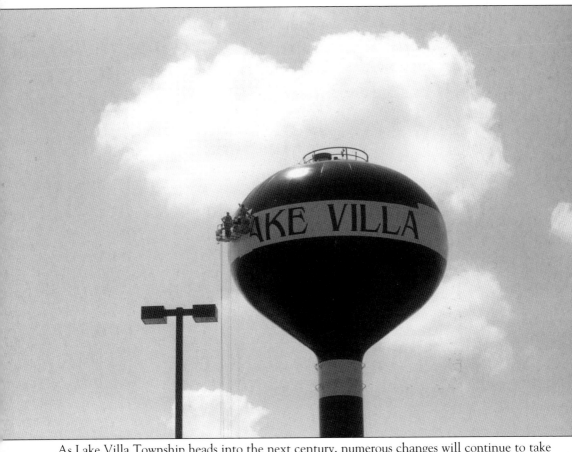

As Lake Villa Township heads into the next century, numerous changes will continue to take place. As the Chicago metropolitan area expands, the township will be faced with choices as to how best redefine the community. Zoning codes, public debates, and petitions—these are the tools of a community attempting to take proactive measures towards the future development and identity of the township. Though residents often disagree on the best path toward the future, it is the active mind, the thoughtful action, and the willingness of spirit that will best aid the vibrant township. (Photograph by author.)